"*The Upskilling Imperative* offers a remarkable amount of insight into how knowledge and learning can be unleashed in an organization. Every leader hoping to build or maintain a successful learning culture within their company should read this book!"

—**Marshall Goldsmith**, *New York Times* #1 bestselling author of *Triggers, Mojo,* and *What Got You Here Won't Get You There*

"It's time for individuals and companies to recognize that we must never stop learning. The way to survive and thrive in today's world is to learn—again and again. In *The Upskilling Imperative*, Shelley Osborne not only makes the case for continuous learning, but provides an action plan we can all adopt."

—**Diane Flynn**, CEO of ReBoot Accel, Udemy instructor on Growth Mindset, and author of *The Upside*

"Keeping up with the rapid pace of change is an uphill battle for many employees. Yet learning, upskilling, and just trying to stay relevant has never been more important than right now. How can companies today best support continuous learning and development for employees? With *The Upskilling Imperative*, Shelley Osborne maps out exactly how we can infuse our workplaces with a learning culture that will fuel performance, boost success, and add more meaning for companies and employees alike."

—**Ginny Brzezinski**, coauthor of *Comeback Careers*

"In a workplace with five generations, there's one skill that's important no matter your age: continuous learning. *The Upskilling Imperative* is a road map for anyone who wants to build learning into the flow of work, foster growth throughout every stage of an employee's career, and ultimately use continuous upskilling as a competitive advantage."

—**Chip Conley**, Airbnb Strategic Advisor for Hospitality and Leadership and founder of Modern Elder Academy

"In today's workplace, employees want to grow on the job—up, down, and sideways. Companies that will thrive in today's world of work take professional development personally, and are creating a culture where learning is valued. *The Upskilling Imperative* makes the case for learning as the way we grow and transform as individuals and organizations. Just about every page has an idea that you can put to use right away to make your workplace more human and be more productive."

—Erica Keswin, workplace strategist and author of the
Wall Street Journal bestseller *Bring Your Human To Work*

"Every top performer I ever meet always has one thing in common: they're lifetime learners. Rather than settling after formal education, they embrace a love of learning for the long run. Shelley Osborne's *The Upskilling Imperative* gives a fresh and honest take on how organizations can harness that mentality and cultivate top performers every day."

—Josh Linkner, *New York Times* bestselling author,
tech entrepreneur, venture capitalist

"With the excruciating speed with which work, and learning, is changing—automating, shifting to machines, disrupting every part of our lives—creating workplaces of rich, diverse, perpetual learning is no longer an aspiration. It's a moral imperative. We owe it to those who've served our companies well to prepare them for the future and to keep our enterprises viable and thriving. Osborne and Witkin, and their Udemy team, have done a marvelous job in this book providing a blueprint for how to do it. Scrap everything you thought you knew about what learning really is, and start over by reading this book. Learning is a consequence of thinking and being, not teaching. *The Upskilling Imperative* will guide you on your journey to real learning if you have the courage to follow."

—Ron Carucci, Managing Partner at Navalent and author of
Rising to Power

"When employees think about learning and development, they typically picture a workshop or program that aims to inspire, motivate, and educate—and rarely does any of those. And yet, organizations are still offering them, and employees are still attending them, costing both of them time and money. Why? *The Upskilling Imperative* not only answers that question, but offers fresh and actionable insights into how we can change the learning game into one where everybody wins. Written for readability and packed with relevant research, this book should be top of mind for anyone charged with helping people get better, faster."

—**Deborah Grayson Riegel**, CEO and Chief Communication Coach, Talk Support and author of *Overcoming Overthinking*

"We're going to live to a hundred! Or more. That means lifelong learning isn't a nice to have, it's a necessity—for individuals and organizations. In her new book *The Upskilling Imperative,* Shelley Osborne, Vice President of Learning at Udemy, provides practical advice along with psychological research (on why certain methods work) and the science behind successful sales (so you can market educational opportunities) to demonstrate that democratizing learning is the key to organizational inclusion and personal empowerment. It's a must-read for learning and development professionals and the people enlisting their services."

—**Melanie Katzman, PhD**, author of the #1 *Wall Street Journal* bestseller *Connect First*

THE
UPSKILLING
IMPERATIVE

5 WAYS TO MAKE
LEARNING CORE TO
THE WAY WE WORK

SHELLEY OSBORNE

VP, LEARNING AT UDEMY

AND **PATRICIA WITKIN**

New York Chicago San Francisco Athens London Madrid
Mexico City Milan New Delhi Singapore Sydney Toronto

1 2 3 4 5 6 7 8 9   LCR   25 24 23 22 21 20

ISBN: 978-1-260-46668-3
MHID: 1-260-46668-X

e-ISBN: 978-1-260-46669-0
e-MHID: 1-260-46669-8

Library of Congress Cataloging-in-Publication Data

Names: Osborne, Shelley, author. | Witkin, Patricia, author.
Title: The upskilling imperative : five ways to make learning core to the way we work / Shelley Osborne, VP of learning at Udemy and Patricia Witkin.
Description: New York : McGraw-Hill Education, [2020] | Includes bibliographical references and index.
Identifiers: LCCN 2020007040 (print) | LCCN 2020007041 (ebook) | ISBN 9781260466683 (hardback) | ISBN 9781260466690 (ebook)
Subjects: LCSH: Occupational training. | Employees--Training of.
Classification: LCC HD5715 .O83 2020 (print) | LCC HD5715 (ebook) | DDC 658.3/124--dc23
LC record available at https://lccn.loc.gov/2020007040
LC ebook record available at https://lccn.loc.gov/2020007041

CONTENTS

FOREWORD

I n our world, competition is fierce, and the nature of the work we perform changes fast. To thrive, we need to get back to the most fundamental of all human skills: the ability to learn. Small problem: Many of us have been habituated—through our organizations, those around us, and society—to believe that learning officially ends with formal education. We're unaccustomed to the scariness (and the thrill) that comes from starting at the beginning again and again.

That's where *The Upskilling Imperative* comes in. I love Shelley Osborne's message that learning must be continuous and prioritized. I'm in absolute agreement that investing in upskilling is the path to better performance, better organizations, and more meaning in our work.

I study an incredibly diverse set of organizations around the world, from high-end boutiques and restaurants to bustling chains serving millions. Most recently, I've focused my attention on "rebel talent"—rule breakers who change the nature of their work, their organizations, and their industry, sometimes with spectacular results and sometimes less so. One key attribute shared by successful rule breakers is the willingness to courageously and continuously learn. You can't just rebel; you need to draw on skills to devise solutions and keep pushing until you succeed. Through continuous learning, we channel our inner rebel to push past our discomfort and grow our organizations and ourselves.

I first met Shelley at an event where we were both speaking, and I was immediately struck by how Shelley drew in the audience. In her book, she does the same. As someone who studies and prizes authenticity, I love Shelley's voice. She's encouraging, pragmatic, and clear. And she's the right messenger to get us all on board with spending time every day pushing ourselves to grow.

Make no mistake: it's not easy to make learning part of our every day. Shelley's book, however, will help each of us do just that. It's full of the very best kind of advice: straightforward and supremely doable ideas that you can put into practice right away—and that will make an actual difference.

—**Francesca Gino**, Harvard Business School professor and author of *Rebel Talent* and *Sidetracked*

ACKNOWLEDGMENTS

My husband, Tom: My original editor and thought partner. Relentlessly willing to give me feedback and help me be my best. Also happens to be my best friend. Thank you for encouraging and believing in me.

My family: My mom and dad, my brother and sister-in-law.

Patricia: I am so incredibly honored and will be forever grateful to have worked with you on this book. You gave your everything to will this book into reality.

Shannon: You believed in me and this book from day one, and you made this book possible. Thank you for always having my back and making me better every single day.

Devon: For being a "clutch" performer, as usual and always. I would literally be lost without you, and I trust you with my life.

Every teacher I've ever had (particularly Mr. Kilarski for my first lesson in growth mindset) and every student of mine—child and adult (who were also my teachers).

My Learning Team: For joining me and creating this culture of learning together. It is a privilege to work with each of you.

All Udemates everywhere: The most earnestly authentic, smartest people working at a place where I am challenged to do my very best work.

Jenn Farris: For teaching me that my voice has power and encouraging me to use it for its highest and best use.

Darren: For changing the trajectory of my career, from the original opportunity to work at Udemy and every opportunity since.

For everyone who contributed to this book: I am inspired by all of you and learned so much from each of you.

McGraw-Hill.

Canada: Yep, the whole darn country.

INTRODUCING THE ERA OF CONTINUOUS LEARNING

Up until a few years ago, there was a simple pathway from school to work. You graduated, found a job, and never really needed to look back. For better or worse, life is no longer that simple.

The "future of work" is already here, and front-loading your education is not enough to launch a career, let alone sustain it over decades. We've entered the era of continuous learning, a new way of working that requires all of us to rethink how we view our jobs, our skills, and ourselves.

In Part I, we'll talk about why now is the time to bring learning into our workplaces, better understand what it takes to learn something new, and explore why getting comfortable with change is a necessary ingredient for building a learning culture.

1

Why Are We Talking About Learning at Work?

O ur lives, inside and outside of work, have changed. Automation and machine learning are infiltrating more industries and changing (or eliminating) more job functions. New technologies are evolving more quickly, challenging workers to keep up if they want to stay employed.

At the same time, employers find themselves having to devise new strategies for closing their own skills gaps, developing (and retaining) adaptable workers, supporting upskilling efforts, and preparing workers for whatever comes next. But most aren't there yet.

Meanwhile, employees find themselves in unfamiliar territory. They don't know which skills they should be learning, how to demonstrate their competencies to supervisors and hiring managers, or how to ensure they're really retaining and applying newly gained knowledge. These working professionals may be years out of school and no longer consider themselves "in learning mode." Even recent grads have fears and doubts about what it means to be lifelong learners in a work setting.

Nevertheless, these individuals will have to embrace learning, become more adaptable and proactive, and, essentially, *learn to learn.* This is what we're talking about when we refer to the upskilling imperative.

The good news: we're at our happiest and most productive when we're growing and developing!

Out with the Old

Estimates indicate that a career launched today could last as long as 50 years.[1] Meanwhile, skills stay relevant for only about five years.[2] Do the math and it's clear: we all need to be learning continuously or risk falling behind and having our skills become dated.

Smart companies respond to this trend by doing more to help employees navigate winding career paths and gain the skills that will keep them moving forward. Not simply a "nice" thing to do, supporting employee learning and development is a proven business driver.[3]

Still, learning and development (L&D) programs themselves need to evolve with the times as well. Traditional training approaches were built for a world we don't live in anymore and are even less engaging for twenty-first century workers accustomed to consuming digital content on their own terms (see Table 1.1).

But even more than modernizing the L&D experience, companies need to transform at every level into learning-driven organizations, where working and learning are inextricably linked.

TABLE 1.1 Old vs. New Training Modes

WHAT OLD TRAINING WAS LIKE	WHAT LEARNING MUST BE IN A LEARNING CULTURE
Static, quickly dated	On demand, self-driven
Scheduled, mandated by Human Resources	Intrinsic part of work
One-way push	Democratized across the organization
Completion as proxy for learning	Up-to-date, relevant content and experiences
Programmatic, episodic	Anticipatory

A True Learning Culture Is Democratized

Learning can't be reserved for only those employees of a certain rank or tenure. Consider the message that sends: only some people's growth and development are worth investing in. That's a surefire way to kill enthusiasm and impede results.

But everyone also has to stay accountable and has a part to play in the culture's overall success. Table 1.2 is a snapshot of what that means at different levels. We'll explore this idea in greater depth later in the book.

TABLE 1.2 Accountability for Learning, by Job Title

Individual Employees
▪ Commit to developing a growth mindset; don't be afraid to make a mistake
▪ Bring the culture of learning to your work
▪ Share your experiences with others
▪ Advocate for your own learning needs
▪ Don't fall for myths, e.g., you can only succeed with one "learning style"

Managers and Teams
▪ Embrace your role as career guide for your direct reports
▪ Experiment with social learning, peer-to-peer learning, and other formats
▪ Work to develop a team with balanced skills, where individuals complement each other
▪ Give honest, constructive feedback—and receive it graciously

Organizations (Human Resources, Chief Learning Officer, Chief Executive Officer)
▪ Put employees in the driver's seat
▪ Hire for learning agility and growth mindset
▪ Make it safe to learn and ask for help
▪ Think like a marketer to get people excited about learning
▪ Build the infrastructure to make it work
▪ Signal the importance of learning

A High-Level View of a True Learning Culture

Learning is not something that can happen outside of work anymore. Things are moving too fast, and employee needs and wants vary too much, especially with five generations soon to be in the workforce at once.[4] One recent survey commissioned by my company, Udemy, found that 51 percent of employees said they would quit a job where they weren't offered necessary training,[5] while millennials in particular cited learning and development opportunities as the second-most important benefit, after salary, they expect from an employer.[6]

Historically, training initiatives have come out of the L&D or human resources (HR) departments. That needs to change. While the L&D team should serve as facilitators, individuals, managers, and organizations share responsibility for building, upholding, and participating in the learning culture.

Here are the main components for a successful learning culture, which we will explore in greater detail later in the book.

1. Develop and Foster Agile Learners

When leaders embrace change and are open and adaptable to what comes next, they position themselves and their teams for the twenty-first century workplace. As a foundation for creating a culture of learning, leaders must help their employees develop into agile learners who embrace change and growth. To create agile employees, organizations should empower individuals to access learning resources in their moment of need, even as those needs change and evolve, and then allow people to engage with learning when, where, and how they prefer.

There are numerous elements of the learning agility puzzle—coaching workshops, career development conversations, durability principles, and the like—that can be done to support individual learning that is specific to a team, role, or stage in the employee life cycle. For leaders, it's time to think differently about their responsibility to build the organizational muscle for change and foster a workforce of agile learners.

2. Feedback Is Fuel for Learning Cultures

In a work culture that celebrates personal growth, people should feel safe to share honest, constructive feedback with colleagues. And they need the time and space to think about feedback they've received and what they can do to improve.

This isn't about telling someone what they're "bad at" and then telling them to fix it. Instead, the objective is to maximize strengths and encourage people to become their best selves. Indeed, people stop putting forth their full effort if they believe others will accept nothing less than perfection; it has to be okay to talk about our mistakes.

To be clear, this is decidedly *not* the same as going through performance reviews. For starters, learning, feedback, and reflection coexist and should be happening all the time, not according to a company-mandated schedule.

Rather, organizations need to normalize feedback and build reflective structures into how people work. They need to provide training that helps people understand how to give and receive feedback and make room for people to reflect during their day.

In addition, individuals need to get comfortable asking for and hearing candid feedback. As I like to say, feedback is fuel! Without open channels, you won't know where you have opportunities to grow.

3. Think Like a Marketer to Drive Learning and Development

Years of poor training initiatives have caused employees to consider workplace learning a necessary evil, rather than a professional imperative. As we all know, when a product or business has a bad reputation, the first step is for marketing to swoop in and educate the market. It's time to channel that same mindset to rebrand learning and create a tangible culture around it.

Thinking like a marketer is a chance to get creative with learning, but it's also a way to take a customer-centric approach that resonates with employees' needs. The best way to retain learners is to understand their needs and wants, get creative about how you engage them in learning experiences, and market to them before, during, and after learning or training to keep them interested.

4. Put Learning into the Flow of Work

A learning culture doesn't just happen by magic; it needs to be created and nurtured in each employee. It starts with a companywide recognition that we all can and should want to continue growing; we are never "finished" with learning. Needing to learn isn't viewed as a weakness or deficiency in such an environment. On the contrary, it's accepted as a natural part of the career journey and a sign of self-awareness.

One of the most important tenets of the learning culture must be that access to professional development opportunities is democratized throughout the organization. No one should need to have a certain job title or tenure to take full advantage of available opportunities.

All employees should know they have the freedom and opportunity to learn whenever they need or want. They should also be empowered to decide what they should be learning and how.

Understanding that not everyone is a naturally self-driven learner, the organization needs to put mechanisms in place to encourage learning and make it desirable. Managers need additional training so they can help their direct reports discover their learning interests and guide them to the best resources.

5. Signal the Value of Learning

Although more and more companies now recognize the upskilling imperative, they're not exactly sure how to act on that information. Traditional training programs have left corporate leaders skeptical about investing more time and resources into initiatives with unclear outcomes. They're looking for new approaches that see significant employee engagement and improved performance without disrupting productivity.

At the same time, individual employees know they need to gain and maintain new skills but aren't always sure where to start or how best to do it. Or, they may not work for organizations that support their learning needs or connect them to useful resources. This is a stressful place for workers with many years of employment ahead.

This book lays out the business case for why a learning culture is the answer to the many challenges posed by rapid technological change facing every company, team, and individual. From there, we will see how some real people and companies are taking action and leveraging learning as a strategic asset to:

- Close the skills gap
- Retain head count and attract new hires
- Improve engagement and job satisfaction
- Spur innovation and cross-team collaboration
- Move more quickly and nimbly

● ● ●

Harnessing the power of learning isn't as simple as rolling out more training modules or sending people off to a bunch of workshops. It takes careful thought, planning, and commitment. But, when done right, the culture of learning you create will yield benefits at all levels and position you and your team for future success.

2

What Have We Learned About Learning?

All organizations have to evolve to serve modern workers in a culture of continuous learning. But let's first review why, specifically, traditional training programs are no longer adequate for today's learning needs.

Historically, "workplace training" has had a bad reputation. And it's not like this is a closely guarded secret. Just do a search for "bad corporate training memes" and you'll see what I'm talking about.

So, why do so many of us have negative associations when we hear about employee training?

- **It's mandatory.** Of course, certain compliance trainings really *are* mandated by law, regulation, or policy. They're the soggy, overcooked vegetables no one likes but everyone has to choke down. However, some companies go further and make other types of training compulsory. Any learning experience that's rolled out uniformly to everyone is ultimately going to be useful to only a few. You can't take shortcuts if you want engaged, motivated learners; so, no, you can't create one-size-fits-all content.

- **It's boring, static, passive, and outdated.** There's a reason lots of stock photos for "corporate training" show dead-eyed workers slumped at desks. Too much learning content feels as if it was created in another era, long before we became accustomed to interactive online experiences, on-demand video, and the countless sources of information (and entertainment) competing for our attention at work and at home. Do you really think an audience accustomed to the sensory feast of *Avengers: Endgame* is going to sit still for a tedious PowerPoint presentation?

- **It's punitive.** In some instances, training has been inflicted on employees who need to "fix" a shortcoming. Too often, performance reviews and evaluations are used to zero in on what employees are doing "wrong," particularly in cultures where mistakes are viewed as personal failures rather than opportunities to learn and improve.

- **Training is doled out as a reward.** In this case, only the "good" employees get to go. This is a broken narrative. Learning has to be seen as a must-have for all. Every employee, every level.
- **Outcomes of training are not always clear.** When the outcomes of training are unclear or not compelling, senior executives question the value of investing in them. As a result, any training that does exist is a low-priority afterthought, and it feels that way for employees who have to sit through it.

Taking Learning and Development to the Strategic Level

Despite training's dreary history, don't fall into the trap of jumping from "training is broken" to "learning is pointless." Learning isn't the bad guy in this story.

We—management and employees—need to give HR teams the chance to show us they can have a bigger impact. At the same time, we must also acknowledge that L&D and HR aren't one and the same, even if some of the personnel overlap.

The demands of the twenty-first century workplace require different approaches. It's not about doing more. It's about doing L&D better. So, no more mandatory, one-size-fits-all training sessions that interrupt the workday and force people to sit through boring content. Training has to be delivered in ways that make sense for busy workers who are used to consuming digital content all the time. That means self-paced, on-demand, and video based, preferably in bite-size chunks, so people can apply what they've learned to whatever they're working on right now. And when you gather people together, make it worth it.

Moreover, we've learned a lot more about what makes for effective learning. The challenge is moving those insights from the learning science realm into the corporate setting. Don't worry, you won't have to become a PhD to accomplish that.

A Brief Foray into the Science Behind Learning

I started my career as a high school teacher in Canada and spent almost a decade in the classroom, mostly teaching Spanish and English. Like most people brand-new to a profession, I made mistakes. Lots of 'em. I remember spending hours inundating my students with material from overhead projector notes while they literally sat in the dark. Yes, *an overhead projector* (Figure 2.1). I had no idea what I was doing, I had no time to prepare my lessons, and I was pretty much on my own to figure it out.

It didn't take too long to see that my approach was not engaging my students or helping bring any of my teaching material to life. I came up with other methods and modalities that made more sense for my students, and pretty quickly I started to see actual learning taking place.

FIGURE 2.1 OMG, remember this thing? How many of my students were asleep?

(Cherie Speer)

So, imagine my surprise and confusion when I transitioned to corporate training and discovered the learning function was still stuck in that overhead-projector mentality. In fact, there were a lot of lessons I had learned the hard way from my classroom days that fit perfectly into the office setting. Ironically, when I moved from teaching high school to the private sector, a well-meaning manager advised me to keep my teaching background on the down low; otherwise, my corporate colleagues might see me as "soft" from having spent so much time around children. I was also told my teaching experience "didn't count" in the business world. (Ouch, that hurt.) But in short order, I found the situation to be just the opposite. Now, I am quite happy to talk about my classroom experience when I meet new employees, stand in front of a conference audience, or consult with corporate customers. It's an important piece of my own career journey, and it is completely relevant to my place heading up L&D inside a learning company now.

Learning and development professionals, like everyone, are busy people moving fast. That doesn't always leave much headspace to reflect on whether some ideas and approaches could be improved and updated. Sure, it will take hard work, but it will also open opportunities to show how workplace learning can make a strategic impact.

A ton of time, research, money, brainpower, and curiosity is put toward understanding how people learn and how we can use that science to improve traditional education experiences and outcomes. But, as I've discovered, we don't become a new species of learner when we move out of the formal classroom and into the world of work. Following are some of the lessons I've brought with me from my high school teaching days that resonate strongly with my corporate learners.

Lesson 1: Necessity Is the Mother of Learning

Completion cannot be taken as a proxy for learning. In fact, checking boxes was *never* an accurate reflection of effectiveness. Training programs must have a clearly defined goal, measurable outcome, practical application, and ongoing value and relevance. Employees should never walk away from a course or workshop thinking they're "done."

People retain knowledge when they have an immediate need to apply it and ongoing opportunities to reinforce it. That's why it works so much better for employees to seek out new skills when a real need arises that's personally motivating, for example, gaining a new competency to succeed on a project or show they're promotion ready.

FIGURE 2.2 Hermann Ebbinghaus's forgetting curve

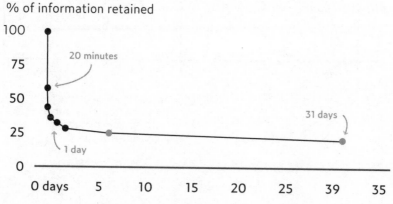

(Atlas, https://www.theatlas.com/charts/H16nE-jvM)

The German psychologist Hermann Ebbinghaus first researched and demonstrated the "forgetting curve" in the nineteenth century (Figure 2.2). Basically, he found that people forget most new information right away. But he also discovered people could retain more if they repeated the new information at regular intervals—that is, "spaced repetition."[1]

Beyond the finding that spaced repetitions produce more learning, neuroscience also reveals that longer spacings tend to produce more long-term retention than shorter spacings.[2]

FIGURE 2.3 Learning and forgetting with spacing on the job

% of information retained

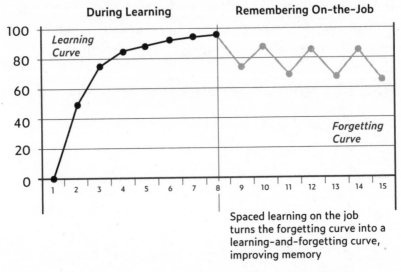

(William Thalheimer, *Spacing Learning Events Over Time: What the Research Says*)

When people recognize their need to learn and continue using a new skill, they'll see the benefit of repeated exposure and practice (Figure 2.3). Learning and development can establish the structures that empower an employee to engage in learning and repetition, but the student has to identify and prioritize what's driving his or her need in the first place.

We're often stuck thinking that spacing has to be as long as or as deep as that first touchpoint of learning, but research from Thalheimer again shows us that's not necessarily the case. We don't have to repeat a three-hour workshop to get the same value from the learning. We can explore the concept in new and different ways. He suggests that repetitions of learning points can include:

1. Verbatim repetitions
2. Paraphrased repetitions (changing the wording slightly)
3. Stories, examples, demonstrations, illustrations, metaphors, and other ways of providing context and example
4. Testing, practice, exercises, simulations, case studies, role plays, and other forms of retrieval practice
5. Discussions, debate, argumentation, dialogue, collaboration, and other forms of collective learning

The biggest takeaway is that we need to space out learning points, and to time learning events and spaced practice—whatever type it may be—as closely to the practice as possible.

Lesson 2: Pedagogy (or Andragogy) Must Be Prioritized over Novelty

Like every other line of business, L&D and HR people have their share of jargon, and they sometimes fall for hype and jump on shiny new trends just because they're getting lots of buzz. Emerging technologies like virtual reality and augmented reality have exciting potential for learning, but L&D practitioners shouldn't rush to embrace them without having solid instructional design and content first.

Indeed, a lot of what we've learned about learning is that concepts we used to accept as truths are no longer viewed as valid. It's not a bad idea to see how new ideas and technologies play out before deciding they're right for your team. Consider the concept of learning styles. For 30 years, teachers heard that every student had a preferred style of taking in new information—visual, verbal, auditory, and so on—and that, if instructed using the "wrong" style, the material wouldn't stick. Then, in 2009, the Association for Psychological Science published a report debunking the research behind learning styles and declaring its conclusions not credible.[3] Does that mean you should wait 30 years before adopting a new technology to be sure of its veracity? Of course not. But we all need to do our homework before introducing new technologies and tools.

No less a tech luminary than Bill Gates has said we shouldn't assume technology holds the solution. As he told the *Chronicle of Higher Education*, the approach of simply giving students tablets or other devices to use in their existing environment has a "really horrible track record."[4] Richard Clark, professor of educational psychology and technology at the University of Southern California, published a definitive study showing that pedagogy (i.e., teaching practice), not medium (i.e., technology tools and resources, such as whiteboards, handheld devices, blogs, chat forums), makes all the difference in learning effectiveness. Clark asserted that instructional media are "mere vehicles that deliver instruction but do not influence student achievement any more than the truck that delivers our groceries causes changes in our nutrition."[5]

Here's the point for corporate trainers and instructional designers to keep in mind: You must start with a crisply defined learning goal. Then, choose the best delivery method for achieving that goal. That might be a slick tech interface, but it could just as easily be a social learning program that consists of employees simply discussing a topic and learning together.

Lesson 3: You Are Responsible for Creating the Energy in the Room

I stole this one from Oprah Winfrey, but as is so often the case, she said it best: "You are responsible for the energy that you create for yourself, and you're responsible for the energy that you bring to others." Standing in front of a classroom of teenagers: so true!

There's a lot you can do to set the right mood in the physical spaces where learning happens. Effective L&D can't take into account only the training content itself; you have to consider environmental factors that contribute to or detract from successful learning. This includes everything from the physical space itself (room layout, temperature, music, lighting) and materials presented (slide design, participant guide, handouts) to attendees' bodily needs (snacks and breaks) and emotional considerations (relationships, anxieties).

Not surprisingly, many of us find it hard to stay alert and engaged when we're trapped inside a bland conference room for hours or days on end. It even makes a difference what the room temperature is, whether there are windows, what colors are on the walls, and so on. One study found a 26 percent increase in performance on math and reading tests among students who were exposed to more natural lighting.[6]

I've carried over a lot of helpful nuggets from the classroom to the corporate training room. Here's a little more about each:

- **Physical layout.** Are you trying to facilitate independent work? Breakout groups for collaboration? Discussion among the entire audience? Might there be employees engaged in different parts of the training but still in the same room? All those considerations will affect something as simple as how you arrange tables and chairs.
- **Music.** My team actually creates playlists to get learners in the right headspace before the session begins, to keep them energized during break times, and to wrap up at the end on (literally) the right note.
- **Presentation materials.** When confronted with endless, jam-packed PowerPoint slides, people's eyes glaze over. It's not their fault. Our brains can only handle so much cognitive load before we tune out. In short, if it takes too much effort for us to process and store information, we won't learn successfully.

Smart instructional design can ease the cognitive load on learners by taking into account the very real limits of our working memory. Distractions take a huge toll on our cognitive energies, which is why you should ban smartphones and even computers if they're not required for the training.

Strong instructional design also creates the conditions for powerful learning. As a teacher, I was introduced to the concepts of scaffolding and the zone of proximal development. The latter concept, credited to psychologist Lev Vygotsky, addresses the gap between what learners can achieve on their own and what they can achieve with encouragement and guidance from an expert.[7]

Vygotsky's work also asks us to think about how we layer and build out information to teach others. To ensure learners are supported throughout the process, we have to meet them where they are, add to and acknowledge their existing knowledge, and guide them through expanding on that knowledge. Scaffolding is a great metaphor for the ancillary activities led by a trainer or subject-matter expert to support students as they navigate the zone of proximal development. Scaffolding is like training wheels on a bicycle that keep riders upright but can be removed once they've gained the confidence and competence to ride independently.

As my team will attest, I also pay close attention to the look of the learning content we create. It doesn't matter if we're producing online video-based courses, slide decks, or handouts, we strive to follow design principles that are conducive to learning.

I'm a huge fan of communications expert Nancy Duarte and her books on visual presentation design. I keep ordering more and more copies of her *slide:ology: The Art and Science of Creating Great Presentations* as new people join our team because her design principles help us ensure that learning efficacy takes center stage and is bolstered by the design.[8]

I'm also a sucker for incorporating a symbolic visual motif to deepen the learning. Our self-advocacy workshop uses a Rosie the Riveter theme to convey the idea of empowerment, and our Career Navigator workshop riffs on mountain imagery to represent peak career experiences. These visual metaphors create memorable and positive associations for students as they revisit and reflect on what they've learned.

Lesson 4: Fear Is the Learning Killer

Okay, an Oprah quotation is no surprise, but how about author Frank Herbert offering up this wisdom in his sci-fi classic *Dune*: "Fear is the mind-killer. Fear is the little death that brings total obliteration."

As I've mentioned, not everyone approaches learning activities with confidence and enthusiasm. Linguist Stephen Krashen studied the factors that affect someone's ability to learn a new language, and one of his hypotheses was around the so-called affective filter. If a student's affective filter is up because they're embarrassed or feel judged, Krashen posited, his or her ability to acquire language is constrained.[9]

This is just one more reason that L&D must start by building relationships based on trust throughout the organization. I learned this as a language teacher, as I saw students shutting down out of fear, embarrassment, or anxiety. I took great pains to reduce those feelings—telling stories of my own language learnings and focusing on small achievable goals.

These same fears and anxieties appear in the adult setting and can often be amplified. We're done with school now, right? We're supposed to have it all figured out. But when people feel that spotlight on them, the feeling that they don't know something can shut down the conditions for learning. Great L&D practitioners understand this and know they need a high degree of emotional intelligence to stay attuned to how learners are feeling and how to interpret what they're saying and what they're *not* saying.

But fear doesn't have to come from within. Here, I'm specifically talking about high-performance work cultures in which people believe they're expected to be perfect. They are afraid to take risks and fail publicly, so they play it safe and try to stay out of trouble. Learning cannot happen under these conditions.

Companies have to create a culture in which it's okay to make mistakes—and talk about them. That comes from encouraging a growth mindset in every employee. I'll explore more about this foundational work of Stanford University professor Carol Dweck in Chapter 5, but the gist is this: We all have the capacity to learn and grow, but we have to understand that it's a process, not an outcome or goal. We only improve when we push through the discomfort of trying, failing, and trying again. Dr. Brené Brown says something similar: Letting yourself be vulnerable takes courage, and it can be painful. But when you get up again after a setback, you grow and you get better.

If yours is a culture dominated by fear, where employees are reluctant to speak up about problems and challenges, people won't be able to learn and develop.

Lesson 5: Don't Make a Fish Climb a Ladder

Last quotation for now, this one often attributed to Albert Einstein (not everyone agrees), and it gets thrown around a lot in education circles: "Everyone is a genius. But if you judge a fish by its ability to climb a tree, it will live its whole life believing that it is stupid."

Regardless of who said it, it's true, and it's important. We can't measure all our learners by the same criteria, nor can we deliver on their learning needs the same way. Individuality is our strength, so let's not fight it. Sure, there are occasions when you want the whole organization swimming in the same direction. You're probably well aware of those. But you'll quickly discover—when you're making connections and forming relationships, when you get responses to your posttraining surveys, when managers regularly have career development conversations with their direct reports—there are many instances when our individual differences need to drive the experience.

When we think about how to develop our employees, the focus needs to be on strengths, not weaknesses. Psychologist Abraham Maslow developed the hierarchy of needs to describe the stages of human growth (Figure 2.4). You're likely familiar with this theory, which has reached the mainstream as the mindfulness movement continues to gain steam.

At the top of Maslow's pyramid is self-actualization, which is the idea that individuals seek to be the best versions of themselves. We get there via continuous self-improvement. But as the hierarchy shows, other conditions must be satisfied before we can achieve self-actualization. For example, we first need to feel safe, have a sense of social belonging, and believe in ourselves. As we'll discuss, L&D practitioners are instrumental in fostering workplace conditions that will satisfy those needs.

FIGURE 2.4 Maslow's hierarchy of needs

(SimplyPsychology.org, https://www.simplypsychology.org/maslow.html)

Maslow also formulated the theory of having peak experiences,[10] moments of pure joy felt by those who've achieved self-actualization. Individuals having a peak experience will feel that they:

- Have lost track of time and space
- Are a whole and harmonious self, free of dissociation or inner conflict

- Are making full use of their capacities and capabilities and reaching their highest potential
- Are functioning effortlessly and easily without strain or struggle
- Are totally in command of their perceptions and behaviors
- Are without inhibition, fear, doubt, and self-criticism
- Are spontaneous, expressive, and "in the flow" of whatever they're doing
- Are open and receptive to creative thoughts and ideas
- Are present in the moment and uninfluenced by past or expected future experiences
- Are experiencing pleasant physical sensations

Peak experiences sound awesome, don't they? But when we ask fish to climb a ladder, we're taking them away from the place where they can shine and, therefore, away from self-actualization and peak experiences. As L&D professionals, we can't ignore areas that need improvement, but we also have to let a fish be a fish.

For example, it's reality that career paths are no longer linear. People are exposed to a lot more opportunities and options, and it's perfectly acceptable for people to decide they're interested in pursuing something different from what they're doing now or what they once aspired to. What is an L&D practitioner to suggest to an eager, motivated employee who wants to move into a new area of work?

At Udemy, our own product uses artificial intelligence (AI) and machine learning to recommend what courses employees should take now—and take after that. These recommendations are based on trends and behaviors exhibited by other platform users who've expressed an interest in the same learning topics. We can even match them with instructors similar to others they've liked in the past.

It's now within our reach as L&D professionals to facilitate personalized learning experiences using tools like differentiated instruction (tailoring experience to individual needs) and adaptive learning, powered by technologies such as machine learning and AI.

Don't force a square peg into a round hole, and don't make an employee sit through sessions that are irrelevant or out of context.

Lesson 6: Learners Need to Put Some Skin in the Game

It's a challenge to keep students fully engaged over the long haul. To do that, you'll need to get creative with rewards and incentives for extra motivation. Gamification is a topic near and dear to me (I wrote my master's thesis about it), and it works when done right.

We weave gamification into many of our initiatives at Udemy to encourage people to put some skin in the learning game. As members of a learning company, of course, our employees are more predisposed to pounce on L&D offerings than workers at other organizations, perhaps, but that doesn't mean we don't have to work for it too.

Gamification is often oversimplified to the idea of giving out prizes or turning everything into a competition, but it's much more than that. Gamification is the use of game mechanics and experience design to engage and motivate people to change a behavior or achieve a goal. That might mean developing an actual game—which is something we have done at Udemy and will discuss in Chapter 6—but there are other, less obvious ways to gamify a learning experience to make it more compelling and engaging. In fact, plenty of products or apps you use every day leverage gamification techniques.

Software companies have gotten particularly good at gamification. I've always been a fan of BJ Fogg, the founder and director of the Stanford Behavior Design Lab, and his work on persuasive technology. He talks about how technology can adapt or motivate a behavior, which is a useful way for L&D practitioners to think about how to begin designing gamified experiences. Fogg also came up with his B = MAP model,[11] which examines how motivation, ability, and prompts must work in concert to produce a behavior (Figure 2.5).

When we design gamified learning experiences for employees at Udemy, we think about the behavior we're trying to instill. Then we dig deeper into our learners' motivations and abilities to determine how strong a trigger, or prompt, is needed to produce action. As Fogg concludes, we need to think of all these factors together to influence behavior.

I also like Yu-kai Chou's Octalysis framework for gamification,[12] which identifies what he calls the eight "core

FIGURE 2.5 Fogg Behavior Model

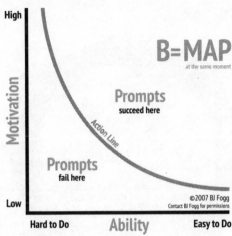

(BJ Fogg, BehaviorModel.org)

drives" of human motivation (Figure 2.6). These include things like meaning (finding greater purpose), accomplishment (overcoming a challenge), and social influence (wanting to match or outperform others). It's important for leaders to understand these drives in order to provide the right motivation for the individuals on their teams.

Understanding each individual's motivations is critical to designing learning experiences they'll connect with. Another way to think about motivators is how Richard Bartle breaks game players into four archetypes: killers, explorers, socialites, and achievers. These might sound familiar from the last game night you had with friends or family (especially if you were playing Monopoly). Someone at the table was absolutely dead set on winning; they're the killer. And someone else really just wanted to be with everyone and kept losing track of when it was

FIGURE 2.6 Yu-kai Chou's Octalysis gamification framework

(Yu-kai Chou, www.yukaichou.com)

their turn to play; that's the socialite. The person who was gutted when they didn't beat their last score or reach a certain game level is the achiever. Last, a fourth player just wanted to get all the way around the board—the explorer.

My team thinks about BJ Fogg's model, Yu-kai Chou's motivation drivers, and Bartle's player types as we seek to understand people's motivations and how we can provide the right triggers within learning experiences appropriate to their ability level. Who are these people? What player type are they? What will motivate them to change their behavior?

Here's an obvious and classic example of how we bring all this to life at Udemy. In addition to regular performance and career goals, we ask Udemy employees to set learning goals. They can earn raffle tickets for entering their goals into our system, achieving their goals, logging the most learning hours, and other behaviors and milestones. We give out much-coveted raffle prizes, like high-tech suitcases, elaborate fancy-food gift baskets, generous Amazon gift cards, and more. Top learners get a cool hoodie that says, "I'm kind of a big DEAL"—a reference to our Drop Everything And Learn motto. Believe me, people want those hoodies and will work to get one.

Now, that's all the stuff people immediately think about when they hear "gamification." People get prizes; this must be a gamified experience. And it's true that people are motivated by cool prizes; raffles prompt them to engage in order to win, and that's how we nudge the behavior of continuous learning.

But gamification is also layered far deeper into our instructional design. When we designed our new onboarding course, for example, we used these frameworks to create a fully gamified experience. We designed both a course and an augmented reality experience. The video-based course was just that—not a game at all. But we still thought about player types and motivations and ended up building the course as a "choose your own adventure," where folks could learn what they needed, when they needed it.

Yu-kai Chou's framework influenced how we built our employee onboarding. We focused on meaning and empowerment as the likely motivation drivers for new employees. With that in mind, the company's mission and the employee's role in fulfilling the mission became core themes woven throughout the program. As a result, we saw phenomenal completion rates for the course and significant increases in how quickly new hires achieved productivity.

We also built a game—yes, an actual gamified game. Inspired by *Pokémon Go*, we created an augmented reality scavenger hunt called *Udemy GO* that challenged new employees to get into teams and collect knowledge about Udemy. We'll get into the development process for *Udemy GO* later, but the socialites and killers were thrilled with this opportunity to win the game and meet new Udemates.

Lesson 7: You Don't Learn How to Swim in a Library

As lesson 5 pointed out, context is king. When I taught Spanish to Canadian high schoolers, I organized trips to Spain and Cuba for them. It's one thing to sit in a classroom in Alberta and practice Spanish; it's a whole other thing to immerse yourself in a culture where Spanish is the prima lingua. I knew this firsthand because I didn't learn to speak fluently until I had spent time studying in Spain myself.

And, as lesson 1 explained, we don't learn unless we're in the position to have spaced repetition and actual on-the-job opportunities to practice. Yet so much of typical corporate learning is event based. This is where we need to follow a communicative-language teaching approach.[13]

Traveling to Spain didn't automatically turn my students into Spanish speakers; I had to push them to interact with native speakers to become truly conversational.

You don't achieve language fluency by learning to conjugate verbs or memorizing vocabulary lists, or my students would have accomplished the same thing back in Alberta. But it's useful to share the theoretical underpinnings of a subject before sending people off to practice in the real world. My students wanted to be able to do things like read the menu and order a meal in a Spanish restaurant or communicate with new Spanish friends. That's exactly the practical experience they gained while in Spain.

It's not all that different with professionals in a work setting. Managers want to know how to delegate effectively, not just talk about frameworks for delegation. Trainers have to find that balance between theory (the "why" behind a particular approach) and practical application (the ability to accomplish things that are relevant and meaningful). Plus, starting with theory will lend credibility to whatever you explain next.

Another thing to keep in mind when you're teaching working adults is Malcolm Knowles's theory of andragogy.[14] Although I borrow many lessons and insights from my time in the classroom, I have to acknowledge what's different when it comes to L&D at a company. Knowles studied this and concluded that, when you're instructing adults:

- They need to know *why* they should learn something.

- They learn by doing (experiential).
- They see learning as a way to solve problems.
- They learn best in the moment of need.

● ● ●

So, yes, we've learned a lot about learning, and many in L&D need to unlearn the antiquated ideas and approaches that have soured so many on corporate training. No longer does the L&D instructor possess the knowledge and choose when and how to share it—that is, the "instructivist" model of learning. Today, especially for adult learners, we need to shift to a "constructionist" vision, where learners own and control their experiences, thereby investing themselves personally in the process and retaining more knowledge over the long haul.

3

Building a Learning Culture Means Getting Comfortable with Change

Understanding and accepting that change is constant, necessary, and positive is the key factor for thriving in the modern workplace. I refer to this sense of adaptability as change agility, which is all about seeing change as an ongoing opportunity, not as a threat or liability.

That's easier said than done, but when you embrace change and are open and adaptable to what comes next, you're positioning yourself and your team for the twenty-first century workplace. The consulting firm McKinsey &

Company equates this sense of adaptability with "lifelong employability: helping people continually and successfully adapt as the economy evolves."[1] McKinsey also found that many companies are far behind in restructuring themselves to operate with learning as a core capability, despite the fact that "75 percent of executives said they believed reskilling would fill at least half of their future talent needs."[2]

Why is adaptability key for organizations and individuals? First off, it's simply too expensive for companies to hire their way out of the skills gap, that is, the growing delta between the skills that employees possess and the skills employers want.

Second, hiring top talent, especially in areas like engineering, machine learning, and data science, has become increasingly competitive. The cost of attrition is rising, too; by one estimate, "it costs employers 33 percent of a worker's annual salary to hire a replacement if that worker leaves."[3] It can take a long time to find the right match, and even then, employers may lose out to other companies offering better compensation, benefits, working conditions, and so on. In the meantime, your business is still lacking those critical skills.

Not only does adaptability have a huge impact on an organization's bottom line, but it also turns out that employees are craving this skill and growing more vocal in their demands for professional development. They're already feeling the urgency to keep their skills updated and relevant in a fast-moving workplace, and they believe employers need to support them in this effort. Research by Udemy found that 84 percent of US workers think there is a skills gap and more than a third (39 percent) already feel personally affected by it.[4]

Developing Change Agility

You know what it's like: You hear about an impending change at work, big or small, and your mind starts racing to what that might look like and how it could affect you. Or, suddenly there's a new tool or technology you have to master to stay competitive. You might worry about not having control over your situation. This stress preoccupies you and prevents you from doing your best work, which definitely won't help matters.

Learning teams must go beyond helping people gain the expected established skills. We need to be present to help professionals succeed in their careers, which takes all kinds of competencies and even coping skills. This is where change agility comes into play for every organization. My call to action for the entire learning community: step up, think differently, and embrace our role as building organizational muscle for change.

Embracing the Reality of Continuous Change

Agility isn't how we've traditionally talked about learning in a work context, but we know L&D has to evolve to serve modern workers in a culture of continuous learning.

As discussed in Chapter 1, we all need to be ready for a five-decade career. Organizations must foster agile workers who adapt seamlessly to change, and we can only do that by learning continuously.

Other factors are also contributing to the need for change agility and continuous learning. The modern workplace is more fluid than ever. Career paths are no longer linear and predictable. Workers may find themselves moving into job titles that didn't exist when they started out.

Although I'm definitely not a neuroscientist, I always follow news and research in this field with intense interest. There's so much we still don't know about how the human brain functions, and I'm fascinated by every advance in our understanding. From my reading, I've taken away five key conditions that individuals, teams, and organizations need to get more agile in the face of change.

THE FIVE BUILDING BLOCKS FOR CHANGE AGILITY

1. **Be Ready for Anything**
   The brain is a helpless prediction machine, Hilary Scarlett tells us.[5] We like information and certainty. Without it, we default to the fight part of fight-or-flight mode. The more the brain can predict and make sense of what is happening, the less threatened it feels. By acknowledging the

inevitability of change, we can stay in the right mindset to roll with it. The L&D team has a key opportunity here to support the development of both situational awareness, where employees can anticipate the change that's coming, and self-awareness, so employees can understand their own reactions and feelings.

2. **Think Outside the Box**
   The human brain is wired to try to conserve energy and conditioned to take the path of least resistance. If we know a way to do some-thing already, why learn a new way? We need to encourage people to innovate and take risks to remain competitive in a given industry. Learning and development can help with simple methods to challenge and adapt entrenched thinking while also identifying the intrinsic and extrinsic value of personal development.

3. **Reduce Subjectivity**
   Reappraisal and reframing techniques have been shown to reduce activity in the parts of the brain connected to emotion, allowing us to view the world more objectively and remove perceived threats. For example, with training around change agility, we can learn to reinterpret events and situations in a constructive light, so that anxiety doesn't interfere with our ability to handle the unexpected.

4. **Tolerate Ambiguity**

   Change often requires decisions to be made swiftly, perhaps also in the face of ambiguity. That can put us in threat mode, and the brain responds protectively by falling back on bias or shutting down in decision paralysis. Decision-making frameworks give people steps and guidance on how to process ambiguity while maintaining progress and productivity. As leaders, we can empower those around us to move forward even without the complete picture.

5. **Communicate in Change**

   We are more comfortable with certainty about a negative outcome than we are with generalized uncertainty. That's why leaders need to become skilled at telling their people what's happening and assure them they'll be supported through whatever comes next. The best leaders are pros at putting context around change and guiding their teams through it. More important, acknowledging a leader's own need to change and develop makes it safe for others to do so too.

An Elevated Role for Learning and Development

In this new era of business agility, L&D hasn't necessarily kept up, because, again, it hasn't been viewed as a strategic priority. Many companies still model workplace learning after what they experienced in traditional classrooms, with the trainer as a "sage on the stage," delivering training employees have been assigned to attend. Others haven't evolved from where they were in the 1990s, when the Internet first emerged and corporate L&D simply digitized existing training content without taking full advantage of what online learning and other emerging technologies have to offer.

Another big factor in the effectiveness of workplace learning (or lack thereof) is the historic approach of the L&D team itself, which sees itself as the gatekeeper of knowledge and the defender of protocol.

HOW PCL CONSTRUCTION HAS ELEVATED HR AND L&D

My first corporate training job after transitioning out of classroom teaching was for a very large Canadian construction company headquartered in Edmonton, Alberta—PCL Construction. As such, it was formative in shaping my ideas around what it means to create and maintain a robust learning culture.

PCL was already a trailblazer in operating according to the philosophy that learning must be part and parcel of everything we do at work. Then, I lucked out in having Mike Olsson, another former classroom teacher, as my manager's boss. Mike is currently PCL's vice president of human resources and professional development, and he shared his thoughts on what distinguishes PCL's learning culture, why it's only gotten bigger and better over time, and what other companies can do to follow their lead.

When Mike joined PCL as an adult educator in 2005, it already had a strong reputation for being a learning culture. "Within days of joining I got a sense of the special environment and commitment to its people," he says. "The culture is driven right from the top because the majority of our people 'grew up' with PCL.

"Also, all of our senior operations people and executives are graduates of our leadership and high-potential programs. They've experienced the growth and transformation that's possible when you go through many of our programs, so they get it and they believe in the investment."

Although PCL is large enough to have a full HR team, Mike explains that "L&D is embedded in HR, so the culture is kind of driven from everywhere in the organization." In fact, all of PCL's HR team members across the organization are actually human resources learning and development (HRLD) people. The two functions are in lockstep. "Our HR managers are relied upon to be facilitators and teachers of many courses and programs, and we have L&D competencies built into our expectations of all HR people," Mike explains.[6] Then there's a corporate L&D team made up of instructional designers, multimedia staff, corporate trainers, the manager of PCL's leadership academy, and various special program managers.

Mike had walked into an organization that already prioritized learning, and so did I when I started working for him. After his first year at PCL, Mike transitioned to be an HR manager for one of the company's small industrial districts. He grew his role in HR while continuing to facilitate, teach, and lead people development programs.

Mike has tips for other companies when it comes to building out their own L&D functions, whether it's part of HR or a dedicated team of its own:

- From the beginning, clarify your organization's values.
- Figure out your organization's *why*.
- Don't make a big financial investment unless the organization is all in.
- Bring in someone who *gets it*! Or look internally. You will need to have a driving force who can align with company leaders to drive the L&D strategy and culture.

We've learned a lot about learning, and we know the way we run L&D has to change. What does that mean from a practical standpoint? Should workplace learning still fall under the purview of HR? Does every company need a dedicated L&D team or person? At what point does a company get big enough to merit the addition of a chief learning officer on the executive team?

The answer: It depends. But no matter what, it can't fall to just one person.

For the Many, Not the Few

One of the crucial first steps to empower change agility is to communicate that everyone "owns" learning. I've seen this work a lot of ways, and much of it will be determined by the perspectives of the executive team and the HR lead as well as the competence of the person running L&D. Although the "learning leader" role can live successfully in many parts of the organization, what's nonnegotiable is a shared understanding that learning is a strategic need for the business, not something that sits on the periphery or is an afterthought.

Bake Learning into the Employee Life Cycle

Learning and development has often been a reactive discipline, happy to wait until it has been requested or asked for. But, in fact, the L&D mindset has to be baked into what HR does to support every step of the employee life cycle. Old models marked development as one phase in that life cycle, but L&D should be woven throughout the life cycle, evolving with the employees themselves.

Added pressures and challenges around hiring and retention in the twenty-first century have elevated the influence of HR. As never before, HR is getting its proverbial seat at the table with the rest of the key business drivers. Learning and development also has to make this move.

Ride the Changing Tides

We've already established that a learning culture is employee-driven. For example, my team works closely with HR on our employee engagement surveys and uses that input to identify gaps in our L&D offerings. One recent survey revealed a strong desire for more diversity and inclusion content, which led to our Manager's Guide to Belonging training. The guide helps managers talk about sensitive topics with their reports, stay alert to DEI (diversity, equality, inclusion) issues, address their own unconscious biases, and work to create the conditions for psychological safety on their teams, all of which are foundational for belonging. But we didn't stop there. We also created a self-advocacy and allyships workshop for individual contributors, so *they* would know how to surface any concerns and be mindful during interactions with coworkers.

In the past I've "embedded" L&D colleagues in various teams around a company to understand how we can serve them better. We also meet regularly with business leaders to make sure they're communicating with us and not pushing learning aside when work gets hectic and stressful.

Depending on the size of your organization, you may decide on the Center of Excellence approach or embed L&D folks as business partners. Both can work, and there are advantages and disadvantages to each. Embedded L&D people can end up replicating each other's work or duplicating efforts, often without knowing it. In another instance, someone may have built an exceptional program, but it only gets used by part of the organization. On the plus side, embedded L&D can be laser-focused on a team's or department's needs, build buy-in, and anticipate opportunities more easily.

Be in Service to the Business

Companies should be less concerned with where learning falls on the organization chart and more interested in creating programs and opportunities that serve the learners and the business itself.

Indeed, my professional L&D mantra is to always be in service to the organization. I learned this lesson before my "real" career even started, though I didn't realize at the time that it would become my guiding credo.

While I was at university, I had a part-time job as a Zamboni driver at a local ice rink. Hey, I'm Canadian! This was a normal job for a Canadian student to have. This meant dealing with beer leagues—amateur teams playing hockey and socializing at the rink—wanting to hang out and drink when I needed to clean and lock up.

They didn't take me seriously. I was just a university kid and "a girl" to boot. None of my nagging and begging did anything to change their behavior. So, I tried a different tack. I got to know them. Instead of being adversarial, I built relationships with these guys. I found better ways of communicating so they would understand my situation. And they came to respect the fact that I was just trying to do my job well and developed empathy. At the end of the season, they invited me to their year-end party and gave me a huge tip for my work throughout the season. This didn't happen for students who had done the job in the past.

I bring the same approach to my professional career. Whether you're in HR or L&D, you can't just be a rules enforcer. You need to negotiate, build relationships, and show people you're not an adversary but someone who wants to help them have a great experience. I recommend flipping the script from "You need to get better at X" to "I'm here to help you achieve your goals. What do you need to achieve them?" You can only establish that level of communication and trust by getting to know people and understanding their needs.

Employees respond enthusiastically when you move away from mandatory training and, instead, invite them to explore, discover, experiment, and grow into new things. Indeed, one of my measures of success is how many people return (of their own volition) for coaching and practice after our initial session.

This comes naturally to me because I also spent years as a high school teacher, where I learned that you don't grow enthusiastic learners by forcing them to follow rules and complete arbitrary assignments.

Trusting relationships create an environment in which people are confident sharing constructive feedback, asking for learning support, and talking about struggles. That openness strengthens relationships, which leads to better outcomes, which leads to better relationships, and so on.

Your Relationships Are Your Insight into Change

I also saw firsthand at PCL Construction that having solid relationships across the company enables L&D people to be more effective in their capacity as change agents by giving them insights into business shifts before they happen. Here's an example. At one point at Udemy, we decided to put three of our biggest departments under a single leader. The change wasn't going to be a seismic shift impacting people's day-to-day work, but I knew from experience that these types of changes can trigger lots of complicated emotions—anxiety, confusion, anger. My team and I had already been planning coursework around change management for Udemy's internal L&D platform, but I accelerated the timeline when I heard this news. As a result, we were able to have relevant trainings available at the same time the changes were announced, and we were able to minimize fallout.

Annual and quarterly goal planning is a great time for an L&D team to be front and center. Rather than simply tell people it's time to set their goals for the year or quarter, our L&D team has a Goal Crushing course that walks employees through the process. We use the same idea for people's personal development goals. My team put together a course called Career Navigator, with versions for both individual contributors and managers, so both parties know how to have effective conversations about where they want to go in their work lives.

The output of these goal-setting sessions is also a great source for me to find opportunities to support the business through learning initiatives. Whatever people put in their goals, that's where they're going to need to develop their skills. These goal-setting conversations are the earliest indicator of where the company's priorities are moving. In addition, we designed our Change Agent workshop to keep up as the business goes through shifts in strategy, structure, and more. Our role as the L&D team is to help people acquire the skills to get through transition times, but we also want to teach them to be change agents themselves.

Nobody came to me and asked for these programs. They came about because we are embedded in the organization and are in constant communication with teams and coworkers about their challenges and objectives. Giving L&D free rein to connect with people around the business, rather than waiting for them to approach HR, lets us see around corners, anticipate challenges, and head off issues before they escalate.

Change Agility Matters for Learning Leaders Too

In addition to strong relationships, another important trait for the modern L&D professional is our own change agility. You can't help employees pivot in response to changing business conditions if you are slow to adapt yourself. This is also where I think the consulting hat fits; consultants are accustomed to adjusting as their clients shift their plans and capabilities. Your corporate clients—employees—need you to roll with the unexpected, too, so they can count on having relevant, effective learning experiences available when they need them.

This is the strategic side of L&D: acting as transformation agents and guiding your organization through times of change. It's challenging, but it's also one of the most rewarding parts of being learning leaders in a learning culture.

Learning and development people also need to be good at promoting their services and programs. In staffing my team, I look for candidates who can "think like marketers" to evangelize learning and drive engagement. Remember, this is no longer about pushing out mandatory training modules, and it's on us to communicate the value of continuous learning and get employees excited about embracing it. It's hard to do that if you're not authentically passionate about learning and helping others gain knowledge. (We'll get into more details and examples of how you can market your L&D team's offerings later in the book.)

Last, and connected to being agile and adaptable, L&D leaders need to think big about today's needs while staying ahead of what's coming next. We can't wait and react to things that have already happened. By staying on top of trends, patterns, and opportunities—both inside your organization and inside your industry—you can know where your efforts will have the greatest impact and, from there, prioritize accordingly. Still, the C-suite has to recognize the value of its L&D visionaries and derive maximum value by elevating L&D to a strategic asset with a seat at the executive table. If you're hoping to land that seat yourself, I'll share more about how to do it in Chapter 9.

FIVE WAYS TO MAKE LEARNING CORE TO THE WAY WE WORK

Part II is where we'll get into the meat of how to make learning an integral part of your organization. I'll share the five crucial elements that define a learning culture. Beyond simply identifying the elements, we'll walk through how to foster them with your employees and teams.

We'll also explore how you can identify and reward agile learning and learners, a new (and more positive) way to think about feedback, and the lessons marketing can teach us for how to drive learning. I'll offer my best practices on how to make learning part of everyone's routine every day and how to give learning and its value more visibility inside and outside of your organization.

4

Develop and Foster Agile Learners

When the key skill for the modern worker is continuous learning, your entire organization needs access to it. That's why the most important tenet of a learning culture is that access to learning should be democratized throughout the organization. There can't be a hierarchy or gatekeeper for who gets to learn.

If organizations expect individuals to commit to developing their growth mindsets and becoming agile learners, management must hold up its end of the deal by creating an environment of freedom, opportunity, and love of learning. Everyone has a part to play in making the culture grow and thrive, and so all employees should also be entitled to avail themselves of all your learning resources.

Learning also must be disassociated from the retribution/reward reputation it has previously had. Continuous learning is core to all jobs now and requires agility.

What It Means to Be an Agile Learner

When I give talks on agile learning, I start by reminding people that their college graduation was referred to as a commencement. As a former schoolteacher, I love the idea that we're celebrating a new beginning, not marking a finale. To me, nothing better reflects the idea of continuous learning than that. You may be moving from classroom to office, but you're certainly not done with learning.

Then, I show my audience the graphic in Figure 4.1.

Even with an educational pedigree that includes Berkeley and Harvard, someone who completed his or her MBA in 1992 never learned anything about today's most commonly used marketing technologies. And don't feel smug if you're a more recent grad; the top curve will keep traveling up and to the right while your formal education gets more and more dated. In 2018, the World Economic Forum estimated that, by 2022, 27 percent of all roles will be jobs that don't exist yet.[1]

Rest assured, your existing job is going to change as well. Hence, the upskilling imperative.

FIGURE 4.1 Can a marketer afford to stop learning?

When are
we done?

● Marketing tools
● Education/training

2017
Snapchat
advertising
Snapchat

2015
Instagram
advertising
Instagram

2014
Account-based
marketing
ABM

2010
Social Media
Management
Hootsuite

2009
#Advertising
Twitter

2008
Marketing
automation
Marketo

2007
Social Media
Marketing
Facebook

2005
YouTube ads
YouTube

1998
SEO/SEM
Google

1995
Internet
Netscape

1990
TV, Radio, Print

1992
MBA from Harvard Business School

1987
BA from UC Berkeley

Learning agility doesn't have anything to do with how good or bad your grades were in school. It simply means being able to figure things out when you're confronted with an unfamiliar situation or problem. On the organizational level, it means operating in a way that empowers employees to access learning resources in their moment of need, even as those needs change and evolve, and then letting people engage with learning when, where, and how they prefer.

Modern Elders Need to Learn, Too

I was fortunate enough to share the stage with Chip Conley during one of my learning agility presentations, and his story brings to life the concept of agile learning in a relevant way.

At age 52, Chip was already a successful entrepreneur in the hospitality industry when he got a call from the much younger CEO of Airbnb, Brian Chesky, asking him to join their team and help guide their growth. Despite his greater years of experience, Chip quickly saw he had as much to learn from Chesky as the Airbnb CEO had to learn from him. Maybe more.

Long story short, Chip was inspired to launch what he's dubbed the Modern Elder movement to evangelize learning agility across the generations and proactively bring colleagues of different ages together to share their knowledge.[2] Some call this a mutual mentorship. Either way, it gets to the heart of what's possible when we lower barriers and open up to learning from each other.

You don't need a formal mentorship program in place, however, to promote learning agility. You just need to socialize the following three questions among your employees and have them ask themselves regularly where their needs and opportunities lie.

1. What have I learned *before*?
2. What did I learn *today*?
3. What do I need to learn *next*?

These three questions bring a level of discipline to our thinking around learning that allows us to reflect and internalize what's happening. When we ask, "What have we learned before?," we're not expecting to dig back to kindergarten. Instead, in this context, we aim to connect knowledge and expertise employees gained previously to the work they're engaged in now or are about to embark on. Get them thinking about past projects that are relatable and how prior experiences can inform current work and make it better.

"What have I learned today?" asks employees to take stock of the moment and to draw learning from both the hits and the misses. Here, we want to help people recognize minipivots they can take to get back on track without having to completely change course. More important, it encourages regular introspection to ensure employees are finding ways to get the most out of their workday and not moving through it in zombie mode.

"What should I learn next?" is a little more complicated. People might get hung up on that final question, and there are plenty of ways the L&D team can guide them to possible answers.

DEMOCRATIZED LEARNING: ACCESS FOR ALL IN THE MOMENT OF NEED

Along with other outdated practices and policies we covered earlier, another big aspect of "traditional" workplace training needs to be retired for good in the name of learning agility. That's reserving learning opportunities for select employees, such as those with fancy titles or with longer tenure.

Employees must be empowered to drive their own learning experiences. Period. When L&D leaders put employees in the driver's seat, they aren't putting themselves out of a job. On the contrary, they'll find they can deliver even more value to both the business and the employees themselves, who are, after all, L&D's customers.

Do you really want a workforce that's only partially engaged in continuous learning? Can you really afford to leave some employees behind?

Hard Skills? Soft Skills? Who Knows?!?

Let's get to my last question for driving learning agility: what to learn next.

When it comes to hard skills, individuals and managers know what they need better than anyone sitting in L&D or HR. Functional leaders watch what's happening in their fields and anticipate which tools and technologies their teams have to get to know. Most engineers read industry news to stay abreast of new programming languages and frameworks. Designers can't fall behind when Adobe changes or adds new tools to Photoshop. Marketers know it's on them to master the latest flavor of email automation. The role of L&D is to provide access and guide the conversation.

But when it comes to connecting employees to soft skills, regardless of their department or years of experience, the L&D team can really shine. Most people have outdated ideas about soft skills, a.k.a. "human" or "people" skills. These are skills like creativity, leadership, relationship building, giving and receiving feedback, managing teams, and so on. It may seem logical to conclude that you're either born good at this stuff or you're not. Fortunately, this idea has been debunked. Carol Dweck's work on growth mindset uncovers that we can improve in all soft skills if we put in the effort and work through our struggles.

The bigger issues when it comes to improving soft skills are that we're not as self-aware as we believe, and we don't always receive the kind of honest, constructive feedback that would give us a clear and accurate assessment of our own soft skills. We don't know we need to work on them, or we don't know they're even teachable skills in the first place. L&D can do more to help managers identify opportunities to build their own soft skills and those of their direct reports.

Laying the Foundation for Continuous Learning

We deliberately devised our slate of courses and workshops to get people thinking about their work through the lens of learning and growth. That starts by training managers to be coaches. And because we teach all employees, but particularly managers, how to give and receive feedback, our managers are equipped with the knowledge and skills to steer those conversations with empathy and good intentions.

Navigate and Coach

An enormous part of a culture of learning is turning managers into coaches and guiding them through the conversations that will entail. At Udemy we double down on both learning opportunities and potential.

To this end, we have made a point of offering two distinct learning opportunities: the Udemy Coach and Career Navigator workshops.

We believe in two overarching leadership philosophies that work together—servant leadership and foundational coaching. A big part of a manager's role is to be in service to his or her team to enhance and level up performance, and that's best achieved through coaching. In the Udemy Coach workshop, we work on eliminating directive and prescriptive approaches, which don't leave room for employee exploration, innovation, and learning, and share coaching methodologies that, instead, help managers bring out the best in their direct reports. Said another way, we help managers empower their teams to grow without telling them exactly what they "should" be doing.

In the Career Navigator workshop, managers learn how to have meaningful career conversations with their employees by reflecting on peak career experiences. Through these conversations, employees better understand what gives them satisfaction, what brings out their best work, and what opportunities are open to them. This workshop is designed to turn every manager into a top-notch career coach, able to partner with employees to help them accelerate their career progression. We deliberately named it Career *Navigator* because it's less about identifying specific job functions and titles and more about exploring the many directions a modern career path can take.

DEAL Hour

Next, you need to give people time to learn. Short for "Drop Everything And Learn," the DEAL Hour designates a specific time when literally everyone in the company stops whatever they're doing for a learning activity. At

Udemy, that typically means spending an hour engaged with any of the courses in our online marketplace, but the L&D team also picks a handful of courses that people can sign up to take together and discuss among themselves. These groups may stay in touch afterward to track how people are applying what they learned and to ask any follow-up questions. They usually have great ideas for the next courses they want to take, too.

One hour a month doesn't sound like a lot, but it's a launching pad to more learning time and a bit of a forced reminder for anyone who hasn't logged into the learning platform for a while. We definitely see increased learning activity after DEAL Hour, as people continue what they started. And that's the message we want to send, whether there's a DEAL Hour in sight or not.

WHEN GOOD LEARNERS BECOME GREAT LEARNERS[3]

Dana Alan Koch, Learning Lead for Talent Research and Innovation, Accenture
Allison M. Horn, Talent Organization Lead, Accenture

Accenture is a leading professional services company, with expertise in more than 40 industries and more than 500,000 employees serving clients in 120-plus countries. We have a deep heritage as a learning organization. Fueling our culture of continuous learning has always been a critical priority—in message, practice, and investment. We invest more than USD 1 billion and more than 30 million payroll hours each year to ensure our people have the skills needed to serve our clients today and tomorrow.[4]

The breadth of knowledge and skills needed to solve today's complex problems and innovate for tomorrow continues to expand. The shelf life of knowledge and skills continues to decline. Our people need to know more, about more things, more quickly than ever before. They need to learn, unlearn, and learn again—across technical, industry, functional, and leadership domains—at a pace that continues to accelerate. Gone are the days when a standardized "one-size-fits-most" curriculum with annual learning requirements comes close to meeting the unique learning needs of a diverse global workforce. Gone are the days when any two people need the exact same combination of learning interventions and support at the exact same time in their careers.

Our old models of "here's a core curriculum, we'll support you through it" no longer work. Yesterday's approaches of "follow this learning path exactly as written" no longer apply. Where does that leave us?

At Accenture, we look to both the future and the past for sources of wisdom and inspiration. To answer the questions above, we stepped way back to the past to find the wisdom to guide us forward, all the way back to a well-known proverb: "Give a person a fish and you feed them for a day. Teach a person how to fish and you feed them for a lifetime."

This proverb is applicable across many contexts, and we apply it directly to learning and development of our people. In years past, we've obsessed over making sure we can provide our people with exactly the right mix of "fish" for their learning. Today, we no longer attempt to serve up the proverbial seafood buffet of perfect learning interventions for our people at every turn. Accenture believes that teaching people to be self-directed, self-guided learners is the true key to success. Rather than telling people what to learn and mandating their completion of learning programs, we focus energy on the skills needed for success and support our people as they forge their own learning paths. Accenture fills its "learning ocean" with a vast array of content and resources for people to find when they need it. Accenture people are adept at "fishing" for their own learning, creating personalized learning paths that focus on the skills they need today and aspire to build for tomorrow.

As a learning and development organization, Accenture focuses on keeping that "ocean" vibrant and ensuring our people have the best "fishing" skills possible through two primary channels, both of which are anchored in learning sciences:

1. Ensuring access to the best learning
2. Creating the best learners

Accenture's definition of the best learning is efficiency based, rooted in learning science, and explained by a simple formula:

Learning Efficiency = Knowledge and Skill Increase / Energy Invested in Learning

Knowledge and skill increase anchors directly to what has been retained that can be used to solve a problem or create a new opportunity in the future. The energy invested in learning includes time, money, and brainpower. *The best learning is the most efficient learning.* The best learning is the learning that helps our people learn quickly in ways that can be applied in meaningful and varied contexts.

Accenture's definition of best learners is also efficiency based. The best learners can find what they need when they need it, and they consume content in ways that work with the natural wiring of their brains. *The best learners are highly efficient learners.* They know how their brain learns best. They apply this knowledge to maximize the energy they invest in learning. They learn more in less time. They reap the benefits through fast, sharp increases in knowledge and skills that help them make better decisions, solve more complex problems, and create new opportunities *at speed*.

Using Science to Create Great Learning

Accenture aspires to be the most truly human organization in the digital age. This requires us to understand human wiring at deep levels and to apply that understanding to create and support organizational structures where humans thrive—both personally and professionally. This includes core human concepts such as connection, belonging, and growth. We are on a journey to understand these core human concepts at both scientific and societal levels across the organization and apply our findings at scale.

A major area of our research is centered on the learning sciences (including neuroscience, behavioral psychology, cognitive psychology, social physics, public health, and education) to understand how the adult brain learns best. We partner with academics and learning ecosystem partners to better understand the actual physiological changes that take place when learning occurs, and to identify ways that we can accelerate those changes through our learning content and structures.

For example, we recently partnered with MIT's Department of Brain and Cognitive Sciences and the Institute for Medical Engineering and Science to study how long people will engage with an instructional video before their minds start to wander, and how engagement can be extended. We tested the power of interpolated questioning on retention. We applied these scientific findings to adjust instructional videos to result in greater retention and higher levels of learning efficiency by changing our approach to the presenter, slide colors, content, questioning levels, and more.

Another example of how we apply learning science to our learning programs is through the application of the right level of stress, which aids in increased learning efficiency. Cortisol is a stress hormone that signals relevance to our brains, alerting us that we need to center our attention. We sometimes build in time limits and other challenges to intentionally introduce productive stress into our learning programs to signal critical points for attention and focus, taking advantage of our human wiring to accelerate learning.

These are two of many examples of how we apply learning science to maximize learning efficiency.

We bring our research findings to life through a pragmatic model we call Durable Learning.[5] This model is centered on eight key principles that enhance learning "durability"—that is, the likelihood that learners will retain and use knowledge gained long after engaging with instructional content. Our L&D professionals are well versed in durable learning, and we share the model with our learners across the company.

Durable Learning: Eight Principles

To maximize learning efficiency, instructional content must be:

- **Relevant.** The class includes instruction that is important to the learner and builds on the foundation of prior knowledge so that learners can more readily integrate it into their work and world.
- **Engaging.** The material gets and keeps the learner's attention. Learning is inspiring and motivational, and learners fully engage and focus.
- **Contextual.** The class provides the "big picture" by leveraging mental models the learner is familiar with and can grasp. Context provides the "hooks" by which new content makes sense to the learner.
- **Effortful.** The material requires learners to actively engage in the learning process and requires their focus and a certain amount of emotional investment. It is challenging enough that failure with feedback is expected.
- **Generative.** This happens when learners put content into their own words. Class material requires learners to draw on their own understanding and make connections to existing knowledge, and it engages both their retrieval and storage memory.

- **Social.** The content engages groups of people in activities, discussions, debates, and dialogues. It often involves discussion from different contexts or paradigms and involves cocreating ideas or deliverables.
- **Practice.** Learning cannot be crammed. The material must be spaced, interleaved, and varied. The class allows time intervals between practice, shifts of what's being studied in between practices, and diverse ways to practice.
- **Spaced.** The learning is distributed over time, allowing learners time to reflect and forget, which requires retrieval, thereby strengthening the learning. Spaced learning doesn't overwhelm or demand too much cognitive load.

These principles continue to evolve with new research and findings. The model is supported by an evolving rubric, which evaluates the durability of both new and existing course designs and offers suggestions for increasing the durability of the learning. As of this writing, the durable learning model has been used to assess and increase the durability of more than 10,000 pieces of instructional content across Accenture.

Applying the Durable Learning Model

Although created and tuned for our needs at Accenture, this model is broadly applicable across organizations of many different shapes and sizes. It costs very little to implement, and many of these principles can be brought to life through small tweaks in existing content.

Pragmatic applications for increasing durability of learning content:

- **More relevant.** Modify course descriptions to emphasize relevance to learner audience, including the WIIFM (What's In It For Me?); hold learners accountable for applying what is learned.
- **More engaging.** Mix instructional approaches; consider using simulations; strengthen faculty preparations to enhance facilitator effectiveness.
- **More contextual.** Add or increase opportunities to reflect on new learning and tie to existing knowledge; practice applying learning directly tied to role requirements.
- **More effortful.** Integrate demanding exercises; use business simulations; ask participants to create something, lead a discussion, or debate each other.
- **More generative.** Have learners "teach back" to peers and/or direct reports; utilize role-playing with coaching; require participants to present the learned materials.

- **More social.** Increase work in pairs or teams; use discussion-based activities; include networking time.
- **More practice.** Provide activities in multiple contexts; ask participants to create a deliverable; add role-playing; integrate quizzes.
- **More spaced.** Integrate blended learning; use the flipped classroom model; add activities that strengthen memory retrieval.

Teaching and Perpetuating the Durable Learning Model Mindset

Durable learning isn't a set of steps or techniques. It's a mindset. To truly make it part of the Accenture learning culture, we invested in helping our partners, sponsors, instructors, content creators, and others understand, embrace, and apply durable learning principles to any learning experience (including town hall meetings, coaching, career counseling, and mentoring).

To that end, we created a set of durable learning cards for the eight principles. Simple and succinct, cards can be used in diverse contexts at the individual, team, and leader levels. Figures 4.2 and 4.3 may inspire you to socialize durable learning principles at your organization.

FIGURE 4.2 The front of Accenture's Durable Learning card succinctly defines the related principle.

Relevant · Engaging · Contextual · Effortful

Generative · Social · Practice · Spaced

FIGURE 4.3 The back of this card explains how relevance holds the learner's attention and fosters information retention and prompts the user to consider next steps.

WHAT?

When content is relevant to a learner, it evokes emotion alerting the amygdala to pay attention and store the new knowledge because it 'is important'. Learners are then able to integrate this new knowledge into their work and world.

SO, WHAT?

Relevance begins with effective guidance to ensure the right people are in the right course at the right time. It continues as instruction leverages real-world problems of importance to the learner. It builds on a foundation of prior knowledge.

WHAT NEXT?

1 What can you do to ensure your content is connected to real-world challenges of the learners?

2 How will you help learners both understand and believe the content is important?

3 What is the role of facilitators in relevance?

DURABLE LEARNING

Using Science to Create Great Learners

Earlier, we introduced the application of the old "teach a person to fish" proverb to learning, specifically to our learners. We are on a mission across the company to bring learning science not only to our learning content, but to our learners as well. This is easy to do. The research is there. The content is there. An Internet search of "learn to learn" will bring back hundreds of ready-to-leverage articles, videos, and online courses that can be used to help good learners become great learners.

At Accenture, we integrate learning to learn content across our learning programs. We do this through custom video series, through prereads for learning programs, through on-stage "power moments" that explain why programs have been intentionally structured as they are, and more. In 2020, we launched a massive digital learning program across the company centered on uplifting the technology quotient (TQ) of the organization, a CEO-level priority. TQ learning launched with learning to learn content as the very first content of the program, making a very visible (and scaled) statement of the power of upping our learning skills as well.

We're Still Learning a Lot About Learning

We know a lot about how the adult brain learns. What we know is easy to apply, and we hope the pragmatic Durable Learning principles outlined here can help you do this for your organization.

This is an exciting time for the learning sciences, and an exciting time to be an L&D professional. Leading researchers believe we know less than half of what there is to know about how the brain learns. It is our responsibility, as L&D professionals, to be active students of the learning sciences and to keep pace with the exciting findings coming out of academic labs. It is imperative that we actively invest in partnerships across corporate, government, non-profit, and academic organizations to accelerate the continued discovery of how the adult brain learns best. There is still a lot to learn about learning. We are ready to keep learning and hope you will too.

● ● ●

Enroll someone in a course and you teach them for a day.
Teach them to learn, and they learn for a lifetime.
—Modern Accenture proverb

5

Feedback Is Fuel for Learning Cultures

The topic of feedback is so important, so foundational, to building a healthy learning culture, it demands a chapter of its own. You must establish a feedback culture before you can achieve any of your goals around learning outcomes and impact. Feedback is the foundation for understanding your own L&D needs and figuring out how best to satisfy them.

The good news is that many companies are already evolving their approach to feedback, and millennials are responsible for driving the change. Millennials are asking for feedback and career development.[1] We should celebrate this. Companies need to value employees who embrace personal growth, pursue big professional goals, and want to understand their career options.

We all need both space to reflect on our own growth and safety to ask for feedback from others. This concept brings to mind a popular quotation (and book title) from executive coach Marshall Goldsmith: "What got you here won't get you there."[2] That's because the work landscape is always changing. Colleagues come and go. Old strategies and approaches may no longer be relevant to today's conditions and objectives. Wherever you hope to go next—with your current employer or another company, in your current role or by pivoting to a different function or team, on your current career trajectory or jumping to a new industry—you'll need to be intimately familiar with your strengths and areas needing improvement. Together, these strengths and weaknesses are the engine that will take you from here to there.

Engines need fuel to operate. The true path to career development is paved with feedback cycles. We need these constant inputs to keep growing and avoid boredom, like filling up the tank with fuel. What's tricky, however, is creating the conditions in your workplace that will make feedback loops take root, so that people don't fear or dismiss feedback but, instead, ask for and apply feedback constantly.

Fundamentals of a Robust Feedback Culture

For too many of us, feedback has purely negative connotations of harsh criticism and a focus on past performance. I'm on a personal crusade to change this and get people to see that feedback is fuel when it is goal oriented, lesson based, and intended to drive growth and future performance.

As a Udemy instructor with thousands and thousands of online students, I have received my fair share of customer feedback. But I've also leveraged my access to this huge "focus group" to ask about their experiences giving and receiving feedback. These students are from all over the world, of all ages and job titles, at every stage of career development, and in organizations large, small, and in between. The trends I've found are telling. Generally speaking, people's best feedback moments were:

- Constructive—honest, tough messages but with the recipient's best interests at heart
- Perceptive, allowing recipients to see themselves in a different way and have real direction about where they should be learning and growing
- Connected to a specific behavior and attached to actionable advice
- From a direct report—it can be lonely at the top and hard to get honest insights from people you manage

- Applicable to both professional and personal life
- From sports or classroom mentors—and people almost always say they're still in touch with those influential coaches and teachers

In his beloved last lecture, the late Randy Pausch, PhD, spoke directly to this need for us to hear honest feedback.[3] Two of my favorite quotations from his talk are, "When you're screwing up, and nobody says anything to you anymore, that means they've given up on you," and "You may not want to hear it, but your critics are often the ones telling you they still love you and care about you, and want to make you better."

What's Been Your Experience Around Feedback?

There's no way around it: when it comes to good feedback, people have to get away from being "too nice" or afraid of hurting people's feelings. However, they also have to commit to sharing only constructive feedback if they truly care about helping someone improve. And they need to receive feedback with gratitude for the person who cared enough to tell them something difficult.

This doesn't happen by magic. To remove fear around feedback loops (and make them helpful, not hurtful), we need to develop an organizational capacity for psychological safety, and that's rooted in the work of the L&D team. We are uniquely positioned to help people build up the "feedback muscle," as I think of it, so they're conditioned not only to receive feedback well but also are proactively seeking it out. With proper training, everyone can get comfortable with two-way feedback cycles to the point where your culture celebrates feedback instead of fearing it.

Understanding Fixed vs. Growth Mindset

Receiving feedback well has got to be one of the most underappreciated and overlooked leadership skills. People think they're better at it than they really are, or they avoid it altogether. But if someone can master the art of receiving honest feedback graciously, they will be unstoppable.

I love the work Stanford University professor Carol Dweck has done around the concept of "growth mindset," which she defines as the belief that "your basic qualities are things you can cultivate through your efforts."[4] She writes, "In this mindset, the hand you're dealt is just the starting point for development."

Organizations can reap considerable benefits by nurturing a growth mindset in their people. According to the NeuroLeadership Institute,[5] in cultures built on a growth mindset:

- Workers have 47 percent higher trust in their company.

- Workers are 34 percent more likely to feel a sense of ownership and commitment to the company's future.
- Workers show 60 percent stronger agreement that their company supports risk-taking.

The opposite is the fixed mindset, wherein your abilities and intelligence are what they are, no matter how hard you work at them. They're innate traits you can't change (Table 5.1).

TABLE 5.1 Fixed vs. Growth Mindset

FIXED	GROWTH
Avoid challenges	Learn from challenges
Give up when faced with obstacles	Persist in the face of obstacles
Effort is useless	Effort is the path to mastery
Ignore negative feedback	Learn from negative feedback, try to improve
Threatened by success of others	Inspired by success of others

You can understand why I espouse the growth mindset; we can all grow and improve. Feedback is the mechanism by which you can discover where those growth opportunities lie—but you've got to be open to it.

Randy Pausch's words, again, apply here. As he said, when people give you honest feedback, it means they care about you and believe in you. So, you should believe in yourself, too—that is, you should cultivate a growth mindset.

Constructive feedback isn't about telling people what they're "bad at" and expecting them to "fix" it. The objective, along with driving business performance, is to maximize strengths and encourage people to become their best selves. Neither is honest feedback the same as a performance review. Learning, feedback, and reflection should coexist and happen continuously, not according to a company-mandated schedule.

It's normal to fear hurting people's feelings, especially when you're going to have to continue working with them every day. On the flip side, you may have encountered someone who had no problem being constantly critical while overlooking the good work people were doing.

Either way, most of us have strong feelings about feedback. And, maybe, you're also carrying some baggage from bad experiences you've had giving or receiving feedback. Regardless of what happened in the past, your growth depends on your willingness to try again. You cannot predict what will happen in the future.

You could also be a feedback hero for others, giving them priceless insights that stick with them over time and help propel them forward in their lives and careers.

In a work culture that celebrates personal growth and supports individuals in achieving their goals, people should feel safe sharing honest, constructive feelings with colleagues. They should also have time and space to think about feedback they've received and what they can do to improve.

How do you prefer to give and receive feedback? What about your direct reports, your manager, and your peers?

It won't come as a surprise that most people want constructive feedback delivered in private, but preferences aren't as consistent around how they want affirming feedback. If you don't know the answers, just ask.

When Someone Is Resistant to Feedback

No matter how fair, diplomatic, and respectful you are, some people simply don't respond well to constructive feedback. The answer isn't to go silent on them. Training can help feedback receivers learn not to react defensively or feel attacked. This comes with developing the right mindset and understanding that personal growth is usually uncomfortable.

You need to work on building trust, and that starts on day one, long before you ever get around to a feedback conversation. When you've established trust, it may still be hard for people to hear tough feedback, but they will know you have positive intentions and are sharing these thoughts because you believe in their ability to grow and improve.

A few tactics you can follow will make the experience more comfortable. For starters, consider the language you use. Even the word *feedback* can trigger people and make them tense in anticipation of hearing something bad. Choosing different words—for example, changing "I have feedback for you" to "I'd love to share some additional thoughts"—can make a real difference.

The best way to get someone comfortable with feedback is to make it part of the regular routine. Separate it from stress-inducing events like formal performance reviews, and engage in feedback discussions on a frequent, regular basis so everyone gets accustomed to giving and receiving. When people are blindsided by feedback, they tend to develop a fear and aversion to this unknown thing that could be lurking around any corner. If you normalize feedback as just another aspect of your working relationship, it becomes as benign as any other scheduled meeting.

And I know whereof I speak. I spent a decade as a classroom teacher, and when I transitioned to being a corporate trainer, all of a sudden I had a boss (and many others) observing me at work. Not only that, but we sent out surveys after every workshop, so I was getting feedback from dozens and dozens of individuals all the time. This was terrifying. I had never been under such close scrutiny or received regular scores on my performance. I dreaded sending those surveys at first.

But guess what: feedback is now my "drug" of choice. It isn't always easy or pleasant to read what people think of me, but it always gives me valuable food for thought and makes my work better. In fact, I wish I had asked for more feedback from my school students.

Another thing that's happened is that, having received a *ton* of feedback over time, I've learned to evaluate it better. I know I don't have to accept every comment I receive. That's an empowering feeling.

There are countless ways to go about spreading the message that feedback is fuel, but it has to be foundational to everything else in your learning culture.

HOW UDEMY BECAME A FEEDBACK-FIRST CULTURE

It's confession time. In the beginning of my career as a classroom teacher, I thought my job was to look for mistakes. I graded tests and quizzes and told students where they had been wrong. That way, my logic went, they could learn the right answers. Then I had an awakening. I realized my job wasn't to catch kids making mistakes; it was to find opportunities for improvement. You can't achieve that kind of growth on the tactical level, correcting errors with a red pen.

As a schoolteacher, I saw how damaging bad feedback could be and have carried those lessons with me to this very day. We all have the power to inflict this on others at work, and we owe it to them to do better. Now, I think about feedback a lot. All. The. Time. And I think about how I can help get everyone else into a natural feedback mindset all the time.

I created my "Feedback Is Fuel" course because there's an art and a science to giving and receiving feedback well.[6] Companies can't simply expect employees to work through tough situations using their gut instincts. Rather, companies should cultivate an environment where it's safe to talk openly about mistakes and where feedback works for both the giver and the receiver.

That's precisely why I created my course—because people can and should learn how to do it right. Organizations need to take deliberate steps to create open channels and normalize feedback to identify development opportunities and set optimal conditions for learning.

We also have to keep it fun and fresh and top of mind long after people have completed the online course. Feedback is certainly a foundation of Udemy's products. We gather customer ratings and reviews to make course recommendations, maintain the quality standards of our marketplace, and identify areas we can optimize. We have tight feedback loops with instructors to ensure Udemy's platform delivers learning experiences that let them reach desired outcomes for themselves and their students. So, the idea that feedback makes things better isn't a foreign concept around here.

We also solicit feedback as an organization through quarterly engagement surveys and Q&As at all-hands meetings. We run hackathons, opportunities for teams to put aside their day-to-day work to collaborate, generate ideas, and quickly solve problems. In many tech companies, hackathons are the domain of engineers, but we don't limit them to only technical teams. We open our hackathons to anyone who wants to engage in discussions about where we can do better as a company, how we can strengthen our culture, and generally, ways we can make Udemy the best possible place to work.

To be clear, we all share responsibility for maintaining Udemy's healthy feedback culture, and each of us has to take the lead on offering, receiving, and integrating feedback on performance, partnership, impact, and results.

Best Practices for Receiving Feedback

- People generally mean well. Assume good intentions, be open to someone else's perspective, and have an attitude of gratitude.
- Accept other people's information as valid, whether or not you agree. Their perception is worth consideration. Don't immediately jump to defend yourself or push back by making excuses or blaming others. Ask for specifics and clarification to understand someone else's point of view.
- Seek out more information, and don't be shy to ask questions. You don't necessarily have to act on every piece of feedback, but give it an honest appraisal. If there are other explanations or mitigating factors, don't feel guilty if it's really not feasible for you to act on someone's feedback.
- Create space for feedback. Get used to it, prepare for it, ask for it, and set the framework. For

example, have your manager give it in weekly meetings, so you know when to be ready for it, where you stand, and what's expected of you next.

- Know what you want feedback on and help your manager(s) and peers give it to you. Send questions in advance, such as, How do you envision our team working together? What could I be doing better? Am I prioritizing the right things? Where should I escalate or not? Am I doing the right amount of work?

Best Practices for Giving Feedback

Where: When you can, have feedback conversations face-to-face. Don't wimp out and hide behind email or chat. Not only is it a bit cowardly, just think about how often misunderstandings happen in those channels—and how easily avoidable they would have been with a conversation in person. Tools like Slack might be great for quick exchanges, but it's no place for sensitive, nuanced discussions. I remember one manager who tried to deliver constructive feedback to a direct report via Slack, and there were so many other messages, emails, and in-person interruptions occurring at once, the direct report totally misread his manager's words. Even worse, he reacted reflexively by telling his teammates he was "getting in trouble," which got the entire team chattering, and then the manager had a bigger problem on her hands.

Electronic communications are convenient, but they're minefields for feedback conversations. You'll save yourself a lot of grief if you and your teammates get comfortable having quick, in-person chats when a performance issue arises. Have your meeting via video or a voice call only when it's absolutely necessary, such as for a remote employee.

When: As soon as possible. Don't store up feedback and wait to dump it all at, say, a periodic performance review. Feedback needs to happen as part of your ongoing routine, so establish regular feedback cycles and allow enough time for questions and follow-up discussion. Schedule weekly (or whatever makes sense) one-on-one sessions with direct reports and use the time to expand beyond status updates; be proactive about sharing and soliciting feedback. Ask, generally, how they're feeling about their work, their development, and their interactions with the rest of the team, as well as what they need from you that they're not already getting. When done right, the rest of the conversation won't feel intimidating or intense, and no one will walk out frustrated or surprised. And encourage your direct reports to do the same—ask them for feedback if they feel they're not already getting what they need.

There's always debate around the best time to deliver particularly difficult feedback. I don't like doing it right before someone goes on vacation or he or she is about to give a presentation. Having a tough conversation first thing Monday sets people up for a bad week, and doing it last thing Friday sets them up for a bad weekend. Find a fair middle ground with enough room for the recipients to absorb and reflect on what you're telling them and to reach back out afterward if they need to. As with everything in life, moderation is key. Keep track of how often you're giving feedback to ensure you don't stray into micromanager territory.

How: You want to create value for the feedback receiver, so come prepared. Be specific and own the feedback, rather than hiding behind generalized statements such as "some people say..." or "everyone thinks..." Be authentic and respectful. This shouldn't be about making demands, doling out punishment, or giving ultimatums, so be sure your intended message is getting through. Ask questions and make it safe for the recipient to speak freely and openly. Then, when you make an action plan together, you'll feel confident you're on the same page, and you'll both feel comfortable with what happens next.

The Darker Side of Affirmative Feedback

It seems like it should be easy, right? Commend someone enthusiastically on doing a "great job," and they'll be nothing but thrilled. Maybe. Can you be sure they'll know exactly what you're referring to? Or might it be heard as vague and empty cheerleading? That's why you need to get beyond simple praise, so people see the *impact* of their positive behaviors.

In addition, listen to recipients and hear their side of the story. You might discover that "great work" is taking a hidden toll. Your high performers might be suffering from burnout, or they actually hated the particular project where they excelled.

I once worked with a stellar new hire who had been rocking it in her first months on the job. I lavished her with praise, then asked how she was feeling. As it turned out, the reason she had been so efficient and productive was that the work was largely similar to her old position, and she was feeling a bit frustrated. She had joined our company because she wanted to learn and grow. She wanted to take on more challenging projects, but her colleagues were afraid of overloading their new teammate. After our conversation, we talked about other areas where she could get involved and contribute.

The Big Takeaway

We all need to be exposed to lots of feedback and learn to get comfortable giving and receiving it. This is just one of the countless "soft skills" in high demand today, alongside critical thinking, conflict management, and relationship building. We can all get better at these skills, regardless of where we are in our lives and careers.

But good feedback doesn't just happen. You need to create the right environment, make a habit of it with regular feedback loops, and work together (giver and receiver) on action plans for moving forward.

6

Think Like a Marketer to Drive Learning and Development

At the beginning of this book, we talked about training's bad rap. We also talked about how people may be carrying negative baggage from their school days and be resistant to workplace learning. At the very least, you're targeting busy people with deadlines and goals that usually feel more urgent than upskilling. And employees, like all busy, distracted consumers, need a reason to pay attention to what you're peddling.

That's why you have to think like a marketer: to cut through the noise, resistance, and misinformation and get people motivated to embrace continuous learning. To drum up interest in L&D offerings and keep people engaged, modern L&D has to be consumer-grade.

It All Starts with Creativity

When I accepted my job at Udemy as learning leader for a learning company, I was presented with two big asks: that I focus on talent development for employees around the world and that I be innovative and creative in doing it.

I'm not sure most of us in HR or L&D think of ourselves as creative people first, but we can and we should. Although I understand how scary it can be to break out of legacy programs you've been doing the same way for a long time, it's also what makes our jobs exciting, rewarding, and fun.

Creativity is a skill, not an art. That means you can learn it and keep getting better at it if you practice. It's all about making connections between things and ideas and your business objectives. You just have to keep asking and challenging yourself, "How do I come up with the new?"

In fact, people often come up to me after speaking appearances and ask me how I answer that question for myself: How do I keep coming up with awesome new ideas? It's not luck or divine inspiration; it's a learned behavior. I have a simple framework I follow to keep my creative juices flowing, and I'll use our reboot of Udemy's onboarding process to illustrate.

Case Study: Taking Onboarding from Boring to Boffo

Onboarding is something we all have to do, but most of us don't do it well. That's what workers say, at least. According to ADP's report *The Human Touch Drives Onboarding Success,* 79 percent of all employees believe the onboarding process has room for improvement.[1] When you're at a company that's hiring and growing like crazy, with locations around the world, maybe it's no surprise that we're not great at making each and every person feel welcomed, prepared, and totally ready to dive into their new jobs.

I admit we faced these struggles at Udemy, too. But where do you start in reinventing something as fundamental as onboarding, something you know like the back of your hand and can't imagine doing another way? Here's how we brought new life to onboarding, by thinking differently, with the help of a five-step framework (Figure 6.1).

Step 1: Consume

As a human being living in the digital age, chances are you consume a ton of content—websites, chats, social media, entertainment, news, books, movies, magazines,

FIGURE 6.1 Framework for creativity

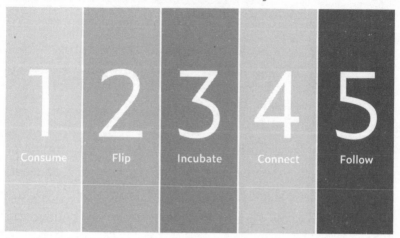

(Udemy)

and more. And what you consume fills your head with ideas and changes the way you think about things. You never know when some article or show will spark an idea you can apply to your L&D programs, so try to bring an active eye to your media consumption and be on the lookout for things that might connect with your learners.

For my team, it was the wildly popular *Pokémon Go* game that triggered an idea for shaking up Udemy's onboarding. The *Pokémon* franchise was conceived in 1989, but in 2016, a new iteration of the game launched for play on mobile devices, and it became one of the most-used apps of the year.[2] Indeed, it was a global phenomenon and the first time augmented reality (AR) technology really entered the mainstream.

I had already been thinking about the potential of using AR and virtual reality (VR) in the learning space to enhance content and deliver immersive experiences. When I gave *Pokémon Go* a try, it sparked a connection for me that I would pursue further.

Step 2: Flip the Script

Creating a mobile game for onboarding sounded cool, but we didn't just want to put the same old thing in a fancy high-tech wrapper. We had to step back first and force ourselves to see things differently by flipping the script. Take a hard, honest look at the status quo and identify what's not working as well as it could be. How are things now, and what could we do to make them better?

In our onboarding example, a few things were broken. For starters, it was eight hours long and boring. There wasn't much interaction, and people weren't retaining knowledge because it was coming at them like water from a firehose. Then, we thought about what qualities we wanted our onboarding process to include: it should use time efficiently, allow for self-driven exploration, incorporate social learning, and promote information retention.

We then translated those qualities into key objectives: to engage employees in our mission, share knowledge about Udemy, and create opportunities for people to bond.

Step 3: Incubate

Too often, we feel pressure to focus on output and completion. We don't let ourselves stop and give our ideas time to percolate. Now, I've already talked about the importance of having time and space for self-reflection if we're going to learn and grow. Well, you need time and space to let your work ideas develop too. So, go ahead and give yourself permission to step back, take your time, go do something else, then return to your reverse brainstorm ideas with fresh eyes.

And if anyone questions why you're using your time this way, you can tell them neuroscience backs it up. I'm sure you've had the experience of having a great idea come to you while you're in the shower or cooking dinner or taking a walk. When we give our brains time to relax and "idle," different areas light up and communicate, which is how we form unexpected connections among the countless ideas in our heads. That's the essence of creativity.

That's how I moved from thinking about AR and VR to playing *Pokémon Go* to being inspired to create a mobile game for the onboarding experience.

I've seen Britt Andreatta speak at a few L&D events, and she does a great job of explaining how the brain generates creative ideas.[3] She emphasizes three important conditions:

- **Rest your brain.** Take breaks to give your neocortex some downtime.
- **Prepare your brain.** Expose yourself to lots of information, especially from unfamiliar sources (because discomfort can be good).
- **Use sensory gating.** Go out in nature, take a shower, or do something else to get a literal and figurative change of scenery.

Step 4: Connect the Dots

I am definitely not espousing technology for technology's sake, as I hope I made clear in Chapter 2. Cool and creative ideas still need to deliver on your learning objectives. Or, as I like to say, you have to prioritize pedagogy over novelty. My Udemy team didn't start out trying to figure out how we could incorporate AR into our L&D programs; we sought to improve onboarding and landed on a solution that leverages AR for maximum results.

That solution was *Udemy GO,* an AR scavenger hunt where players had to catch the welcome balloons we tie to every new hire's desk. Along the way, they were challenged with activities and missions that laddered up to our learning outcome objectives. Not only did this fun experience expose people to information about Udemy's business, but the self-guided nature of the game also empowered players to follow their interests at their own pace, thereby improving retention.

The game also succeeds in making connections (and workplace buddies) among coworkers, as they collaborate on challenges and "visit" our global offices by viewing 360-degree videos and photos.

Step 5: Follow

As psyched as we were about the *Udemy GO* idea, we faced a pretty big obstacle. I didn't know how to build an AR app from scratch and neither did the L&D program associate on my team who was working on this project with me. How would we do this?

As a former teacher, I like to follow other teachers online. The very nature of the job requires them to be resourceful and creative, even though they're always superbusy. They're also constrained by time and budget, something else in common with the team envisioning *Udemy GO.*

By reading teacher blogs, we found a lot of approaches that aligned with what we were trying to accomplish. The blogs introduced us to tools that would let us be creative and fulfill our vision without having to invent something from scratch. We ended up using a free "AR experience builder" that made it pretty easy for us to make a game app that incorporates polls and surveys, quizzes, 360-degree video and photo tours, Snapchat-style selfie filters, leaderboards, and more.

Don't give up on your ideas without digging around to see how others have tackled the same challenges. Both the online and offline worlds are full of people sharing project stories and helpful advice.

The last step in the creativity framework also refers to how we follow up with participants to get their feedback and measure our success. Asking these questions helps us improve our programs and can spark additional ideas we can apply to other projects.

Udemy GO keeps new hires engaged with onboarding content far better than sitting them in a conference room for hours to passively watch presentations. And we have this creativity framework to thank for surfacing the great idea in the first place.

Marketing Your Creative Ideas

Just as you need to have a road map for creating and rolling out your L&D programs, you need to think about how you'll promote those programs—and not just at launch either.

Before you offer any L&D opportunities, you need to set your goals and define your key performance metrics. What will success look like? Who is the target audience for the training and, if it's a broad group, how can you communicate its relevance and value to everyone? You may even want to create "learner personas" to guide your messaging, based on an employee's years of experience, job level, functional area, career aspirations, and so on.

Borrowing Principles from Advertising

Now that you've got creative ideas and a framework for generating more and more, you need to operationalize those ideas.

When you're thinking like a marketer to promote your company's L&D offerings, you're advertising to your audience of learners. You can apply lots of tips and tricks of the advertising trade to move employees from thought to action.

Segmentation

Audience segmentation is a way of ensuring relevant messages reach the right people. Depending on your objectives, you might want to break your audience up by job level, department, time with the organization, or job function. Then, think about the motivators, needs, and friction points of each segment you're targeting and how to tweak your messaging to best communicate the value of your offering to them.

We've found ways to personalize the Feedback Is Fuel workshop (see Chapter 5) using audience segmentation. We survey attendees prior to workshops so we can tailor our content to their biggest needs and interests. The survey includes questions around how often people receive feedback from their managers, how they prefer to receive constructive feedback, and so on. Then, we share that information at the start of the workshop. We'll let people know that, for example, only X percent of them said they want to get affirmative feedback in a public setting or Y percent said they prefer to deliver feedback via Slack. When we get into the meat of our presentation, we can refer back to people's current behaviors and be specific in pointing out possible areas for improvement.

Go Viral

You know what it means if your video or meme goes viral. Everyone shares it, more people see it, then they share it, ad infinitum. Imagine if you could get people buzzing about your L&D programs like that.

When we first began developing the Feedback Is Fuel workshop, we met with the vice president of marketing for Udemy for Business. Our vision was to "rebrand" feedback, from punitive to empowering. The VP helped us position our content and messaging for our audience and talked us through various creative assets to support our launch campaign. For instance, for our launch campaign, we took inspiration from the Mean Tweets segments on the late-night TV show *Jimmy Kimmel Live*, where celebrities read aloud the nasty things random people have said about them on Twitter. The Udemy version is called Mean Feedback and features employees reading questionable pieces of feedback. It connects really well with our audience and it gets laughs, but it also makes people think about how the impact of feedback changes, depending on whether it's "mean" or constructive. We've continued producing new Mean Feedback clips, featuring different employees, so it never gets stale.

Referrals

Building out your learning "fan base" relies on storytelling and word of mouth. Nothing gets Udemates more jazzed about their jobs and the impact of learning than when we share stories about real students and instructors who have succeeded on the Udemy platform. These have ranged from a Syrian refugee living in Germany who was able to secure his dream job after taking Udemy courses, to a Silicon Valley–based engineer who quit his day job after discovering he got more satisfaction and joy from teaching his skills online to other aspiring developers.

We share inspirational stories at our all-hands meetings and on our blog, and we distribute them in external marketing channels and recount them at company events. We also have a "udemy-fuzzies" Slack channel where people share positive comments from students and instructors alike. We even post the best fuzzies in our bathroom stalls.

Real-world stories are the most powerful way of showing how learning truly does improve lives. They inspire everyone at Udemy to keep striving toward our vision of a world in which everyone can find the right teacher, but they also remind us of our own obligation to be continuous learners. And we have ways of surfacing stories of internal learning success too. We've integrated Slack so it's easy for Udemates to share when they've completed a course, say what they liked about it, and recommend it to others (Figure 6.2).

FIGURE 6.2 An example of how we leverage real employee reviews to market our workshops

What are Udemates saying about CHANGE AGENT?

"

Clever, crafty, CAPTIVATING... #changeagent This course had it all. From practical frameworks to role plays as undercover agents **it's my favorite Udemy course I've taken to date!** I loved how everything tied in and you kept us on our toes not expecting what was next.

Teasers

One of the mantras of the L&D team at Udemy is that we "eat our own chocolate." This was inspired by an old expression in software development—"eat your own dog food"—that exhorted employees to become active users of their company's products and services, the idea being that we need to put ourselves in the shoes of our customers if we're going to deliver solutions that align with their pain points.

When we were ready to do a big launch of L&D programs at Udemy, we knew we would attract more flies with honey, so we revised the expression to be about something a little more appetizing than dog food. We left a chocolate bar on every employee's desk with a customized, Udemy-branded wrapper reminding everyone that learning (by taking courses on the Udemy platform, specifically) equals eating our own chocolate.

We also post reminders around the office with fun messaging and visuals to get people talking about our newest courses and workshops. People respond enthusiastically when we get creative with our communications, like the posters we made for DEAL Hour that were styled after vintage travel advertisements and asked employees where their learning would take them. Then, we had a call to action reminding them to participate in DEAL Hour.

Communicate Scarcity and Urgency

This is Advertising 101. You don't just want to get your audience interested in acquiring your product or service *some day.* You want them to do it *now*—before they click away to another browser tab or watch another video and completely forget about you. We, too, try to instill a FOMO (fear of missing out) mindset around learning at Udemy.

You can build anticipation and excitement the same way the geniuses behind hit movies do it: start your timeline a few weeks out with teasers and "coming soon" messaging that hints at something cool people will want to keep an eye out for. This can be done with signage around the office, reminders via chat and email, and speaking slots at all-hands meetings. You know your teasers are working when you hear "water-cooler" conversation about your signage and campaign. Be sure to include clear directions on what steps you need people to take to participate, and clearly indicate the date, time, location, and where to go with questions.

Get a Celebrity to Star in Your Commercial

No, I don't expect companies to have the budget to hire Jennifer Aniston to endorse their L&D workshop. But you do have superstars in your midst—employees known and respected across the organization who can model learning behavior for the rest. Some may come from your most senior leadership; others might be longtime employees regarded as influencers (Figure 6.3). Get your CEO involved; maybe you can use the opportunity to show his or her lighter side too.

FIGURE 6.3 Get employees involved to amplify your message.

Make Giveaways Special

No one is going to be motivated to attend a workshop by a piece of swag that's handed out on every generic occasion. They have a whole drawer full of logo pens and stress balls already. And what does that have to do with learning anyway? Just as you can connect better with advertising that is attention grabbing, you can lure your customers in with the promise of something truly special (and relevant) for everyone who completes the program. For example, at the end of our Career Navigator workshop, we give out branded luggage tags. They fit with the theme of the training, they're something people will actually use, and employees can only get their hands on one by participating.

Follow the Seasons

Advertisers plan around important, predictable events that occur every year, and their customers know it.

Holidays, back to school, spring break, Mother's Day. Amazon invented Prime Day for the very same reason: customers know it will be a good day for them to buy something at the right price. There is certainly a lot of FOMO around Prime Day.

Think about your company's calendar. Do you have recurring events you can use to "prime" people for L&D? You may have performance reviews, an annual retreat, company milestones, or another anticipated event. Use these occasions as another tie-in to push your learning message to the fore.

Retaining Your "Customers"

Getting folks to keep coming back for more might be the most challenging stage of your work. The secret is to continue communicating something new and fresh all the time. Again—not easy.

Sometimes, you can build on existing offerings to give them renewed relevance, such as when we hosted a Manager Lab about giving difficult feedback during performance reviews. This "advanced" class expanded on and reinforced what people learned during the core Lab experience. We also wrote a blog post with five tips for writing effective peer reviews and challenged all employees to use the review setting to talk openly about how they like to receive feedback.

And, I'll be perfectly honest, there's nothing like a yummy bribe to get repeat customers for your learning content. So we give workshop attendees chocolate bars (the good stuff) in a Udemy-branded wrapper. It doesn't matter how senior an employee is, they all get excited by treats and stickers!

• • •

When you think of yourself as a marketer, you can let go and get really creative, but you'll also be taking a customer-centric approach that resonates with your learners' needs. The best ways to retain learners are to understand their needs and wants; get creative about how you engage them in learning experiences; and market to them before, during, and after training to keep them interested and aware of what you have on offer.

7

Put Learning into the Flow of Work

You simply cannot maintain a healthy learning culture if you're not baking it into every facet of your operations. You might be marketing the heck out of your programs, but as any salesperson knows, you still need to seal the deal.

The best way to get people using your product (or learning program) is to make it easy to access and fit seamlessly into the rest of their activities.

Here are some norms you can establish and reinforce to get people comfortable with the idea that, yes, learning is part of their job—maybe even the part they like the most:

- Employees own their learning experiences. No one in L&D or HR can possibly stay close enough to each employee to know everything that person should be learning, let alone how and when. Managers, who supervise daily work and track projects in the pipeline, are better positioned to guide their direct reports, but even then, they need to tread lightly. Employees should have a long leash to balance the must-learn skills for today with competencies they want to build for their futures. This shifts our roles to helping deliver learning at scale, helping managers become coaches, and helping individuals navigate their options.

- Learning isn't an interruption when employees are empowered to pursue it on their own terms. When people are motivated to learn—either by necessity or by curiosity—the best way to maximize that impulse is to give them ready access to the tools and resources they'll need, regardless of subject matter, location, schedule, or learning preferences. A software as a service (SaaS) platform like Udemy for Business fits the bill because it doesn't require employees to get preapproval from their managers but allows them to log in to gain skills in their moment of need.

- Learning cultures enable continuous learning through a variety of modalities. That means people have choices in how they access new information. Online courses are simply one option. Companies should also encourage knowledgeable employees to share their expertise through peer-to-peer learning, and social learning is a great way for teams to learn together and support each other when it's time to apply new skills on the job. Every company has its own resident "explainers," the people who are often called on to teach and simplify what they've already mastered. Explainers tend to be lifelong learners and empathizers. They understand what it's like to struggle with learning something new, and they derive real joy from interacting with students, watching them gain mastery over new skills, and seeing what they're able to do on their own. You would be wise to identify the explainers in your midst and harness their potential for fueling the culture of continuous learning and boosting employee engagement.

- Continuous learning isn't a one-way push, where L&D or others in management are gatekeepers who grant employees access to knowledge. But neither is it a black hole where "anything goes" and no one has accountability for results. Most learning management systems and other digital learning platforms include some level of activity tracking so that, at a minimum, managers can see how people are spending their learning time. Udemy's corporate solution, Udemy for Business, tracks usage and behavior patterns among learners, uses machine learning to spot patterns and trends, and extracts value by leveraging that data to make course recommendations to other users. For example, if we know successful data science students tend to take certain courses in sequence, we can help beginners follow the same learning path to build their own knowledge.

More robust solutions will have activity dashboards with more sophisticated analyses and insights, so you can track entire learning journeys, measure their impact, and use collective data to guide other employees to the best learning resources. For example, a direct report struggling with SQL could be paired with a colleague who's already completed relevant coursework and who can serve as a mentor, sharing his or her own discoveries to make the experience more effective and efficient. The more experienced employee can help the newbie overcome hurdles, show him or her how to apply lessons learned, and recommend other trainings to take next.

Learning isn't something that happens only in workshops or other formal settings; indeed, people retain knowledge better and longer when learning is closely linked to doing.

Focus on Learning in Performance Conversations

The goal isn't just to ensure all employees are weaving learning into their daily routines. It's also about incorporating learning as a subject into ongoing conversations among managers, teams, and individuals. It's motivating to hear about your colleagues' learning accomplishments as well as their stumbles. From a leadership perspective, it informs managers about what skills are represented on their teams, where they need to scale up, and what opportunities are within reach, based on the team's capabilities.

At Udemy, we cover a bunch of valuable soft skills in the programs we've developed around the employee life cycle, in addition to hosting online courses, so that people can focus squarely on one skill at a time. The challenge comes in when managers leave the training room and get back into real-world situations. I like to provide online courses as a reference resources to help managers build skills and refresh what they've learned. One great example of this type of online resource is a course called The Essential Guide for Effective Managers,[1] led by instructor Marie Deveaux, an executive leadership coach who facilitates workshops all over the world.

The employee life cycle topics are available as both self-paced courses and larger workshops. We also recommend people first go through programs like Career Navigator and Goal Crushing to ensure they've asked themselves the important questions and see how learning connects to their long-term goals. These workshops are available throughout the year, but we definitely see an uptick in enrollments when it's time for formal feedback collection.

Here are a few soft-skills-oriented workshops that employees at Udemy have embraced:

- **Change Agent.** To successfully grow as a company, a team, or an individual, we must be able to adapt to change—the good, the bad, and the ugly. This workshop has teams work through escape-room-inspired puzzles as a way of learning five change-focused mindsets (e.g., situational awareness, reframing, projection), so participants walk away confident in their ability to be effective agents of change.
- **Manager Labs.** These workshops are social learning experiences/experiments in which teams come together to share management insights and expertise. We kick these off by encouraging participants to throw their assumptions and biases out the window. Sessions are self-led, and topics are self-selected, which really moves the conversation in unexpected directions and gives voice to ideas that may not have previously found the right forum. Rather than follow a rigid format, Manager Labs are more free-form and expansive to accommodate all manner of input.
- **Bomb Squad.** This is a really fun way for people to understand their teammates and themselves better. First, we run our True Colors workshop, wherein all team members answer a series of questions to reveal how their personal preferences and work styles translate into four different types, each assigned a color (green: analytical, gold: organized, orange: spontaneous, blue: empathetic). Then, we discuss the strengths and weaknesses each color type brings to the table and how to work best with

coworkers who identify more with different colors. We call the workshop Bomb Squad because it culminates with the team playing a virtual-reality game in which they have to use what they've learned about each other to collaborate effectively and defuse a virtual bomb.

- **The Udemy Coach.** One global leadership consulting firm found that 49 percent of workers surveyed want more coaching from their managers, and even more—57 percent—want more external coaching.[2] The Udemy Coach was designed to arm people with skills and techniques so they can serve as coaches to others. It covers topics such as effective questioning approaches and how to develop active listening skills, so that both coach and employee get what they need from the process. We follow the GROW model to guide coaching conversations:

G—What are your **goals**?
R—What is your **reality** in relation to your goals?
O—What **options** do you have, given your reality?
W—What specific actions will you commit to?

Setting Employees Loose to Find Their Own Learning

You can't expect every relevant, appealing learning resource and opportunity to be found inside your own ecosystem of content. Sought-after skills are changing too fast. And you can't create everything you wish were there. It's too time-consuming and expensive, and you'll never keep up. That's why I strongly endorse offering employees a discretionary budget to pay for other approved learning activities, such as attending a conference or external boot-camp or even buying a bunch of online courses, books, or software. This investment is a real and tangible demon-stration of your commitment to employee development and employee freedom to choose.

Employees don't always know how to use their learn-ing budgets, but they know they don't want to lose it. At Udemy, when someone doesn't have an obvious career objective or project need, I encourage that person to use his or her ULearn stipend toward a big stretch goal or to try something really out of the box, even something intimidating. If employees play it safe with their learn-ing budgets, they're missing the point. To be clear, I'm not suggesting companies hand out thousands of dollars to everyone (unless they want to), but the budget needs to be a meaningful enough amount that employees can access a worthwhile learning experience they wouldn't otherwise get to do.

Moving from Programmatic and Episodic to Anticipatory

The resources I've mentioned earlier (Career Navigator, Goal Crushing, and others) are available as on-demand online courses and are supplemented by in-person workshops or blended courses and discussions. They straddle the line between programmatic—activities we host on a set schedule for rotating groups of employees—and anticipatory—always available online resources employees can enroll in whenever they feel the need.

This is the direction L&D needs to be moving: helping people get in front of their learning needs instead of reacting in a rush to acquire a new skill *right now*. You don't need to invest in a crystal ball or hire a psychic, but you do need to strategize and structure your team's offerings to be adaptable and tightly woven into the fabric of daily work as well as the stages of the employee life cycle. There's quite a lot that L&D teams can do to build flexibility into their offerings and encourage forward-looking learning that does more than simply equip employees with skills relevant to the current moment.

Give Them Room to Breathe— So They Can Learn

Perhaps the most critical conditions to have in place to ensure continuous learning are ample time and space to do it. We all have calendars packed with meetings, in-boxes full of unread mail, and incessant text and chat communications coming at us from all sides. Without a formalized, organization-wide commitment to learning, it's almost always going to fall to the bottom of the to-do list after your coworkers' "urgent" requests and work that is deemed "more important" by someone, somewhere.

In addition, people can't give learning the attention and focus needed to make it stick if they're preoccupied and stressed out about all the other things they think they should be doing.

This will take a fundamental shift in how people approach their jobs, and it is definitely going to require more than lip service from the top of the leadership chain. Without that commitment, your L&D efforts won't reach their full potential. And, as an L&D leader, you'll be right back to defending your right to exist. We'll explain in Chapter 9 how to make the business case for a learning culture to your senior leaders, but for now, understand what it means to give people time and space to learn. And how much it matters: according to Udemy's report *What Motivates Employees to Learn*, 54 percent of employees said that having more time would help them learn more effectively.[3]

Help Employees Find Their Learning Happy Place

Programs like DEAL are only one small gesture toward prioritizing learning time. Often, we need to start by helping people "learn to learn" and by offering mindfulness training so they know how to focus and retain information. But first, we need to step back and look at the learning environment itself. I shared some of my learning science lessons about this in Chapter 2, but let's take a closer look at how we can get the details right.

For self-directed learning, it's important that employees can find a space that's reliably free of interruptions and distractions. The American Psychological Association's research found that 61 percent of workers feel their employers provide opportunities for skills development (good news), but only 52 percent say they have enough time to take advantage of those career development activities (bad news).[4]

Setting email and chat to "do not disturb" is a good start. Establishing a dedicated learning space is better, especially when so many of us are in open floor plans where visual interruptions plague us as much as auditory ones. Your company's learning space should be like the quiet car on a commuter train: everyone implicitly understands they need to refrain from talking, silence their phones, and maintain the overall peace and calm of this shared space (e.g., no, you can't bring your stinky lunch or noisy chips to eat in there).

As a facilitator, you also have to pay close attention to your attendees' bodily needs. I've been at this a long time, and I've developed a knack for picking up on cues when people are ready for a restroom/hydration break or a different kind of activity—or that it's time for me to shut up. Yes, I offer snacks and beverages, but they're not just bribes to get people in the door. Science has shown how hunger interferes with school children's ability to learn,[5] but even if we're not dealing with a population that's chronically undernourished, we can still see what happens to learners' attention spans and participation when their stomachs are rumbling. I suggest healthy snacks, like nuts or fruit, instead of simple carbs and sugary treats that lead to a crash later on. You probably didn't expect dietary advice in this book, but this stuff really matters to the effectiveness of your programs.

Finally, it's important to be sensitive to the emotional needs of learners. Obviously, you're not going to do a deep dive into everyone's personal baggage, nor can you expect to know about and accommodate every sensitivity. But you can keep in mind who's in the room and how their working relationships might affect the group dynamic, such as whether they should be paired with others for breakout sessions or, conversely, whether they represent an example of knowledge sharing that others can emulate.

I also remind L&D people and anyone leading a training to remember that not everyone has positive associations with learning. Some of your top workplace performers may have been the most enthusiastic students. For every eager learner with a perfect attendance record, there are others who remember school as a time of anxiety, insecurity, failure, or boredom. People may bring all sorts of feelings, fears, and hang-ups into your training experiences.

Audit the State of Learning

Now that you have an idea of how to integrate learning into the flow of work, we're going to dive deeper into how organizations can audit their learning and ensure it is at the core. I really like the ACADEMIES framework created by McKinsey & Company as a starting point for assessment (Figure 7.1).

FIGURE 7.1 The ACADEMIES Framework from McKinsey & Company

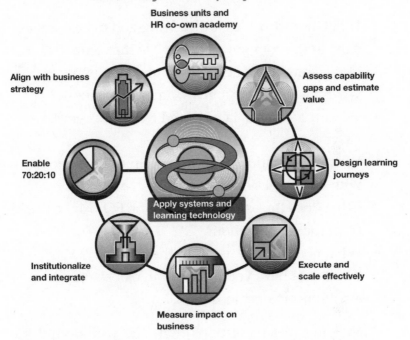

This framework works well for me because it shows learning systems as central to everything and illustrates how every component needs to be integrated into the whole to qualify as a robust learning culture.

Many companies run an annual, biannual, or regularly cadenced employee survey to gather feedback on what's working and what's not within the organization. Explore the following questions as you continue to audit the state of learning in your organization and work toward establishing a true learning culture—whether you're a one-person L&D team, part of HR, or an executive who sees the need to level up your workforce's skills:

- What opportunities for learning and development exist in the company strategy? Is the company doing something new? Looking to get better at what it is doing? Is it growing or downsizing?
- What trends or data emerged from your employee survey?
- What information has emerged in conversations with employees or leaders?
- What does the executive team or CEO want or need from the organization?
- What goals were missed in the past year? Why?
- What data have you gathered in exit surveys or attrition conversations?

Answering these questions will take you around the company to seek out a diverse set of stakeholders and employees and give them a safe, comfortable format for sharing their honest opinions. Then, when you have a clearer picture of the current learning landscape, you can start formalizing a strategy . . . but with one caveat. This data captures only one point in time, and although it's essential to look closely at what has come before, anticipating and preparing for what's next is even more important. Hidden in the answers to these questions will be indicators of where L&D's next steps should lead.

8

Signal the Value of Learning

Everything at your company sends a signal about whether learning is a top priority. It's the job of the L&D team to stay vigilant and keep that steady drumbeat going. Individual employees may not be directly exposed to your team's messaging on a daily basis. How can you be confident people still see your organization's commitment and will keep doing their part to prioritize learning agility?

Leadership signals are the most powerful and impactful mechanisms for spreading a culture of learning. Senior executives can't tout the benefits of learning if they're not engaged in it themselves.

The term *authentic* gets thrown around a lot, but I don't use it lightly. If your leadership team only pays lip service to the core value of continuous learning, you'll end up in a situation where the reality of the employee experience doesn't live up to expectations.

I doubt anyone at your company would deliberately stand in the way of a learning culture; they probably love the idea and embrace it on principle. But it's easy for it to get lost in the daily grind. Research from McKinsey & Company showed a real problem with "short-termism in vital areas such as talent strategy, talent development, and recruitment." Forty-one percent of survey respondents said their companies haven't adopted comprehensive skills training simply because they have "more important things to worry about."[1]

Herein lies the problem: seeing L&D as a separate "thing" from other business priorities. What if, when talking about the important areas where employees should spend their time, leaders spoke of learning agility as the key enabler for tackling those priorities? And those leaders aren't sitting only in the C-suite. You need evangelists and champions across the organization—people like seasoned individual contributors and respected managers whose influence extends far beyond their immediate teams. But without vocal messaging and support starting at the top, L&D's calls to action about embracing learning agility will lack teeth.

When I move around the company doing my listening tours, I'm not just asking leaders to cajole their people to spend time learning. I am increasing my grasp of what learning means for these leaders, what their own story of learning is, and how we can work together to communicate authentically with their teams about building agile learning into their day-to-day routine.

Remember Mike Olsson, my former boss from PCL whom I told you about in Chapter 3? He is an inspiring example of a senior leader who walks the talk when it comes to motivating people at all levels and celebrating learning. It helps that PCL has recognized the value of learning since its early years, having established the PCL College of Construction in the late 1980s, which served as the foundation for all future building blocks.

"The college was as much of a bricks-and-mortar entity as it was a philosophy—a philosophy that supported learning in the company. Importantly, it started with a focus on the soft skills, like communication, listening, negotiating, etc.," Mike explains. "This really meant we were focusing on the person first—before the company. Some very wise PCL leaders knew it was best to invest in the individual, and that company gains would come later, but it was definitely not 'normal' at that time for companies to invest in people first. I believe it was because we were [and are] an employee-owned company."[2]

When Mike describes PCL's learning culture to others in the construction industry, they are naturally envious of such a large organization that has constructed (no pun intended) consistent training programs and an overall culture that's aligned to closely held values and behaviors. Since they've been at it for so long, it's not hard for PCL to correlate the strength of its learning culture to a real and significant impact on business performance.

Yet, even if PCL's learning and development culture is a well-oiled machine at this point, Mike and his team don't take for granted that it can carry on without human intervention. He points to a few of the ways PCL celebrates learning and recognizes achievement to keep the excitement and engagement going:

- Valedictorian award for top student in PCL's leadership course
- Excellence in Construction award, which gives each district the opportunity to showcase great innovations and present them to the rest of PCL
- Regular sharing through internal channels of myPCL stories about culture and leadership growth
- Awards that highlight recipients' leadership qualities in the context of PCL's five leadership practices to signal behaviors and values others can emulate

PCL provides a useful example of how to invest in a learning culture and bake learning into every facet of a business. High-performing companies like PCL are working to align a learning culture with core company strategies and values to succeed in a changing world. The rest of this chapter will share more on the important link between learning and performance and how you can foster that connection in your organization.

Seeing Performance Through a Learning Lens

Another huge signal regarding the importance of learning at your organization is how you evaluate performance at the company and individual levels. Think about how your leaders talk about performance and react to outcomes—the actual language they use.

A company's performance as a whole can also be examined through the lens of a growth mindset, even while pursuing obvious success metrics for revenue, customer acquisition, stock trajectory, and so on. Business strategies need to account for the inevitability of course corrections and incorrect decisions; after all, businesses are made up of people, and people are fallible. Companies can be held back by fixed mindsets as much as individuals can.

At Udemy, we do regular goal readouts and focus on what each group learned from its struggles and successes. On my own team, I ask every member to share a win or a lesson learned, and I start each team meeting by sharing a learning moment or asking someone else to share his or hers. So, it's not just me communicating out to my team; everyone gets a turn, and everyone has a voice worth hearing from. They might share an article, summarize what they heard at a conference, or pass along a tip that might help someone else. This is how we've made learning part of how we operate every day.

My company runs regular engagement surveys to get a pulse on top-level topics, such as how much confidence people have in our leaders' vision and whether employees believe they have a voice in decisions. Because we're a learning culture, we also ask if managers are showing interest in employees' career goals and if the learning opportunities available at our company are adequate. We include an open field for comments too. In our last engagement survey, we got more than 1,000 comments from employees eager to share their thoughts.

The engagement survey is how we learn more about ourselves as an organization. We're pretty transparent in sharing the results because we want every department, team, and individual to take the feedback and apply the lessons learned. We use survey insights to build out action plans that will enrich our learning culture, not to rehash negatives.

It's the same approach when our leadership cohort gets together to discuss the company's performance on the most vital business metrics. Missing a revenue target isn't good, but it can still be addressed from a growth-mindset point of view. This is what I mean about weaving learning into every work conversation: shift the tone from "Here's what happened, and here's what we're going to do next" to "What did we learn from this and how can we leverage the experience to inform future initiatives?"

There are better ways to conduct employee reviews in a learning culture too. You should develop a shared vocabulary to help managers conduct learning-centric performance reviews and career discussions. This is part of my Feedback Is Fuel workshop and the manager trainings we do at my company. By providing frameworks that guide how to talk about growth mindset and learning agility, you can get more out of performance reviews, transforming them from unfeeling critiques to productive exchanges about opportunities for improvement.

Empowering the People

Outside of a formal feedback session like a performance review, an organization can signal in other ways its real commitment to giving employees time and space to learn. One of the most popular new L&D offerings at Udemy has been our self-advocacy workshop. It covers lots of scenarios in which an employee might want to speak up but isn't sure how to go about doing so.

Certainly, given the fears and insecurities we've already discussed, people might hesitate to raise their hands to ask for additional training. This workshop serves as a great complement to Feedback Is Fuel, since learning how to advocate for one's own learning needs is an important part of receiving feedback and pursuing personal growth. After defining self-advocacy and its value in the workplace, this training shows employees how to:

- Discover their communication style and approach
- Practice a method for setting goals
- Identify strategies to communicate more assertively
- Establish when and how to say no
- Find an appropriate sponsor

Don't get me wrong: we don't have this all figured out and perfect at Udemy. At a fast-moving, high-growth company, situations can get stressful and patience can be tested. We expect people to slip into natural postures of defensiveness or aggression sometimes. But, after going through Feedback Is Fuel training, we also expect others to call out behavior that undermines our value of continuous learning and steer discussion back to a constructive tone.

Along with supplemental workshops on self-advocacy and manager training, we hope to give our students tools and techniques that will help them see themselves and others in a new light—one that gives people the benefit of the doubt, assumes positive intent, and acknowledges our collective responsibility to always be striving to learn and grow.

We Need to Talk About Failure

Let's revisit the growth mindset—the belief that we all have the capacity to learn and grow if we work hard and apply ourselves. The harder part to live out is the acceptance that learning is a process, not an event, and that it comes with failures and setbacks along the way. These aren't just hardships to get over; they are integral to our retention and application of knowledge.

When people are afraid of the consequences of making mistakes, they play it safe and stick to what they know. They're less likely to innovate and devise creative solutions that haven't been tried before but hold promise if successful. More than just demoralizing to motivated employees who crave challenges, a risk-averse culture is detrimental to your business results. And yet, according to the global leadership consulting firm DDI, "14 percent of first-level managers we surveyed feel failure is not at all embraced in their organization in pursuit of innovation or different ideas, and only seven percent believe failure is embraced to a very great extent."[3]

We've talked about creating psychological safety around learning. The corollary is making it safe to fail. And not only that, we need to remove the stigma and confront failure head on by talking about it, sharing our stories, and using it as another part of the learning journey. To signal that learning is a priority, the best leaders don't stop at taking courses or finding coaches. They are open in talking about their own failures, learning experiences, growth challenges, and personal goals. They model the behavior they want to see in their teams.

We can all relate to screw-up stories, whether they have happy endings or not. Indeed, some of the most resonant stories are the ones where an individual is penalized or shamed for messing up but then, with time and personal growth, they came to view the episode as pivotal in helping them become the better leader they are today and how they're using that experience to inform how they respond to failure in their current role.

Turning "Failures" into Learning Opportunities

You've got your leaders talking about it, but how do you make it safe to try new things at the team and individual level? And how do you ensure employ-ees really mean it and will support each other through difficult times? Peers can be the toughest critics when someone makes a mistake. I discussed Feedback Is Fuel earlier in this book because it truly is the foundation upon which all else is built. You can't expect people to talk openly and constructively about failure if they hav-en't already learned how to give and receive feedback effectively.

First, look at your vocabulary. I've used a couple of phrases I don't recommend in practice: "screwing up," "messing up," or even "failure." In growth-mindset parlance, these should be discussed as learning opportu-nities. Also be mindful of distinguishing between flawed decisions and the person or people behind them. Flip the script from "You were wrong" and "We failed" to "We learned" and "We know how to do better next time."

Some companies do postmortems after projects to reflect on what worked and what didn't. That's a great start, but it's not enough to encompass your entire work culture. Postmortems are useful for optimizing process, but they don't typically get around to promoting indi-vidual growth. An employee is more than his or her performance on a project. To help people get comfortable talking about and acknowledging failure, those conversa-tions need to be frequent and ongoing. In my L&D team's weekly meetings, for example, everyone comes ready to share a win and a learning.

The commitment to learning can't fluctuate with changes in leadership either. It has to be one of your stated company values, a guiding light for everyone's work that's so baked in as to be almost invisible.

But beware: your company will have to reckon with tension and confusion if your culture purports to value learning but doesn't back it up and sends contradictory messages about failure.

Proactive Managers Promote Learning

The managerial layer of your organization is important because managers are the connective tissue between high-level signals from senior leaders and individual employees tasked with integrating learning into their daily routines. It's one thing to encourage direct reports to approach their managers to discuss their career goals and the areas they want to grow into. It's another thing for managers to get to know their direct reports well enough to share unsolicited learning opportunities that align with those goals.

Younger employees, in particular, may have strong ideas of where they want to develop their careers, but they might not be clear on where to start and how to build on existing knowledge. Managers have to keep their eyes and ears open on behalf of their reports, so their teams can take advantage of new programs from the L&D team as well as external learning opportunities, such as conferences that would support growth.

My Udemy colleague Darren Shimkus is one of our greatest learning champions, and it comes through not only in what he says but also in what he does. He's learned that the key is to tap into something people care about—on an individual level. "Not everyone is going to be an enthusiastic lifelong learner on their own, but I do believe everyone wants to take on new challenges at work and grow their career. But they don't always know how to go about doing that," Darren explains. "I use learning as a bridge to the things they care about."

Of course, Darren can't achieve this from a distance. His management approach is to get to know every person on his team to understand each person's motivations and goals. "You can't encourage any behavior or habit formation until you know what they're trying to accomplish," Darren says.

As the company has grown rapidly, it has become harder for Darren to forge deep relationships with every employee. That's where he relies on the people managers who report to him, with an assist from the L&D team. Manager training includes how to have career conversations and connect employees to learning opportunities that will keep them engaged and excited to come to work. Those conversations filter up to Darren, so he can maintain a holistic view of his team's learning needs and challenges.

Udemy offers two programs that nicely illustrate how this dynamic can work:

- Our Manager Curriculum is offered to help new managers, in particular, adopt the management mindset to engage employees, build a productive and positive team culture, create conditions to promote trust and commitment, and set clear expectations and establish accountability.

- The Public Speaking Club is designed to help employees get comfortable in front of an audience by having them commit to regular practice. The club is limited to 20 participants per cohort, and they meet twice a month to learn as much as they can about public-speaking anxiety, impromptu speaking, and using visual aids.

Both our Manager Curriculum and the Public Speaking Club have open enrollment, meaning anyone in the company can sign up. But people are busy. They may not be aware of every program available or it may slip their minds as they get caught up in other things. This is where a manager can step in to encourage direct reports to participate. If they're having regular one-on-ones that include career discussions, the manager should know which L&D programs align with the report's interests.

When a manager gives an employee the heads-up about a specific program, instead of an employee having to take it upon themselves, it sends another signal that learning is a priority. It says, "Your managers and leaders are looking out for your learning needs here and will actively share opportunities that contribute to your growth." It's not lip service.

We know how difficult it can be as a first-time people manager and how critical manager effectiveness is to employee happiness. We want to give people the tools and know-how to manage themselves, manage their direct reports, and manage the work being done in service to overall business goals. This is complex, multilayered information, and we need to deliver it through a combination of modalities: online Udemy courses, in-person workshops, social (i.e., group) learning sessions, and self-service tools and references.

Although we are still evolving this content, we've already launched our pilot program to the company. It shows that we know where gaps remain in our offerings and how we plan to fill them. It also shows we're listening and taking real action in response to feedback we've gotten through our engagement surveys, performance reviews, and freely shared input.

Prizes, Rewards, and Incentives That Actually Mean Something

Stirring the competitive pot is a great way to retain learners and keep them active in your programs. But the rewards have to be genuinely rewarding. You know what they say: money talks. Small tokens are always a treat, but you can better convey just how important learning is by going big on how you celebrate learners and their achievements.

I've described some of the prizes Udemy gives away when employees hit certain milestones—spending the most time learning on our platform, meeting a personal learning goal, participating in DEAL Hours and learning fairs, and the like. We give away generous gift cards and other high-value goodies, and we also give smaller prizes on a quarterly basis, but we pull out all the stops for our annual awards. First place in our "I'm Kind of a Big DEAL" annual raffle is a $2,500 travel voucher.

I'll point to Darren again because he has inspired such a rich learning culture and brand for himself and his business unit starting when they were still only a team of 10. It started as a joke, moving around a bottle of hot sauce to people's desks at random, then putting it on the desk of someone who had done something great, until that bottle came to embody the team values.

At some point, the bottle went missing. Darren created an official Sizzle & Spice Award but left it to members of the team to decide who gets it. "Our learning culture is also a recognition culture, and there is tremendous value in peers recognizing peers," Darren says.

I love how Darren's team has its own lore and inside jokes and embraces its quirkiness.

But at the organization level, when you're talking about driving a full-blown culture of continuous learning, cheap trinkets can have the opposite effect. Employees may interpret it as a signal the company doesn't take learning as seriously as claimed. You don't need a massive budget, but you do need to be thoughtful about how you can make the biggest impact and send the strongest signal with the resources you do have. One idea I've seen work, especially where funds are limited, is to let the people decide: put the question to your workforce and let them crowdsource the prize or design it themselves (Figure 8.1).

FIGURE 8.1 The Udemy for Business team prefers quirky, homemade awards to traditional trophies.

(Michaela Hawksley)

HOW I SIGNAL THE VALUE OF LEARNING

Darren Shimkus, President, Udemy for Business

I wasn't a naturally engaged student when I was growing up. I was hypercurious but mostly bored with what we were forced to learn in school. But I still appreciated education and found myself learning important things away from the classroom that have stuck with me through life.

My earliest memory of learning was when I was five, and my family had just moved from upstate New York to Maryland. I remember sitting by myself against a tree in our yard looking at a book I had had for a long time. I knew the story from having it read to me, I had learned the basics of phonetics, and I could follow the pictures. But there was one particular day when everything clicked. I read the book and, for the first time, I felt that sense of accomplishment that comes when you figure stuff out on your own. That's a feeling, I think, we all strive to recapture at every stage of our lives.

Later on, when I was a teen, I worked in the kitchen of a nursing home and later had restaurant jobs where I saw the real-world value of getting an education. Our mission was simple: "We make food or people don't eat." I was surrounded by a diverse crew of incredibly hardworking people, some of whom were juggling more than one job in order to make ends meet. Many were immigrants whose own education was limited and who now were determined to send their kids to good schools so they could achieve more in the United States.

Now I lead Udemy for Business, and I'm still evangelizing the value of learning and still pushing the message that it just *feels good* to gain skills, figure things out, and grow as a person. Of course, it's also the surest path to career success. In my role,

I prioritize ways to leverage my leadership role to motivate Udemy employees and Udemy for Business customers to embrace continuous learning.

Not surprisingly, the secret is to tie learning to something people care about. Virtually all people want to take on a new challenge at work, advance in their career, be rewarded for their talents. I use my signal power to create the bridge from those personal goals to the need to embrace lifelong learning. We also talk a lot at Udemy about what it means to have a growth mindset and to understand that learning can be uncomfortable, difficult, and humbling. But the learning process is as important as the learning outcome, hence the need to promote a culture in which it's okay to try and fail and try again.

At the same time, we're not fooling ourselves that everyone is going to be a superlearner, just like not everyone who drags himself or herself to the fitness trainer will become a triathlete. Some of us were unenthusiastic classroom learners; others might fear looking stupid or slow. But I do believe that the energy and attitude of a learning culture are contagious, and when reluctant learners are surrounded by people committed to learning, taking risks, and seeing the results pay off, they'll see the value too. I've sometimes seen the opposite happen in some cultures, where there may be stigma around the need for training. Leaders must make it clear that learning is celebrated as a sign of personal growth and drive, not as evidence that someone is deficient or flawed.

But it's not enough for senior executives to broadcast a blanket message to their whole organization. Team leaders and managers play a critical role here because they are closest to the people who are doing the daily work to keep the company going. Those individuals will have different feelings about learning and will need tailored messaging that speaks to their personal motivations. You can't encourage a behavior change if you don't take the time to get to know your employees as people.

Finally, I think the most important way leaders signal the value of learning is by sharing their own learning stories and by being completely open about what they don't know. First of all, no one is going to believe anyone's claim of knowing everything they need to know and not benefitting from ongoing learning. But more than that, people can relate when you make yourself vulnerable. I talk all the time about what I still have to learn about our industry or certain functional areas. I am totally transparent in saying, "I'm an incomplete work product, and here's what I'm doing to close my own knowledge gap." I talk about my own learning activities, and I implicitly give others permission to do the same.

Something else I've observed: when a leader talks openly about this stuff, you see a trickle-down effect. We spend lots of time in sales team meetings sharing learning stories, and it's really impactful when people hear from their peers and not just the boss. These stories signal that we're about more than metrics and data; we're also about inviting creative ideas and contributions in all forms.

I realize I'm in a unique spot when it comes to evangelizing the value of continuous learning. After all, I work at a company that is literally in the business of connecting avid learners to expert teachers. At a fast-moving organization in a rapidly changing business environment, anyone can get bogged down simply executing the "what" of his or her job. Leaders must get people asking "why" and "how" and then pursuing the learning opportunities that enable innovation and results for both the business and the employees who make it successful.[4]

Creating a Recognition and Reward Culture

Many companies recognize achievement with employee awards, but not all of them host a ceremony to announce them. I know the Dundies, the employee awards ceremony at the fictional company Dunder Mifflin, were played for laughs on the TV show *The Office*, but I am 100 percent not joking when I tell you, Udemy employees get really, really, really into our annual Demmy's award show. We put real budget behind it and, even more critical, we have a team that takes the production seriously.

Preparations start far in advance to ensure that our audience is highly entertained without disconnecting from the night's theme of celebrating learning agility. We make a Very Big Deal over who's taken the most Udemy courses, who's been growing into new skill areas, who's shown the most improvement, and so on. You can tell a lot of love and effort go into producing the Demmy's, and employees appreciate it. In the midst of the fun, there's never any question that the awards are entirely serious about the winners and their accomplishments.

Perhaps the incentive that gets job candidates most excited about Udemy is our ULearn program. Udemy is a marketplace with tens of thousands of online courses, but we would never claim it contains every learning resource a person could ever need. So, we make a monetary investment in every employee in the form of a $1,500 ULearn stipend. We are quite liberal about how this money can be spent. Our employees have attended conferences and workshops, purchased books, and learned new software. The key, again, is helping people make the best use of their learning funds and ensuring managers and coaches encourage their direct reports to take time out to use their stipends.

Reaching Reluctant Learners

I won't pretend that every employee is going to jump on board and become a lifelong learner just because your organization has prioritized it and you've poured your heart and soul into developing fun programs and rewarding those who reach learning goals. Nothing's that simple. But, we should never give up on anyone who is lagging behind in his or her learning activity, and we definitely don't want to penalize an employee who hasn't embraced the learning mindset.

It is, however, totally appropriate for a manager to have a conversation with a direct report who seems unwilling or unable to spend time on learning and figure out what's going on. At PCL, according to Mike Olsson, "When this happens, it is almost always because they are putting the work first; they are totally results focused." Of course, that's not a bad thing either, but Mike cautions that it can be self-limiting.

"Typically, the disengaged learner is someone who's become very successful in their current role. In fact, they do it really, really well," he says. "The issue is that they do not grow beyond this or maybe stall out one level higher." High-achieving workers don't want to hear they're doing something that could stand in the way of their advancement. (To be fair, Mike says it's rare that anyone at PCL doesn't fully embrace the learning culture, given how strong, pervasive, and long-established it is. Few come on board without realizing continuous learning is part of the job.)

Like most culture initiatives, authenticity and transparency from management are needed to build trust and drive companywide adoption of continuous learning. We want *everyone*—at all levels—talking about what they're learning, where they're struggling, and what they would do differently next time, but the example needs to be set by those at the top and communicated regularly and consistently to the rest of the workforce.

In your culture, learning should be like the air itself—it's just *there*, all around. Sometimes you'll deliberately call attention to it, but other times the organization may be sending signals without even realizing it. Stay close to your leadership team to make certain its members send positive messages about learning agility and support their workforce through tangible recognition and rewards that demonstrate their promise to hold learning a permanent priority.

MAKING UPSKILLING IMPERATIVE TO YOUR BUSINESS

Creating a learning culture is rewarding on many levels, from building more resilience within your organization to driving better business results in a changing world. Investing in learning has the potential to transform every business.

While the rewards are great, it's not always obvious how to build the initial business case for learning. In Part III, I'll offer my thoughts on creating the best case for investing in your learning function. And, since the initial business case is just the beginning of the journey, I'll close with thoughts on how you can build a sustainable learning culture so all employees—current and future—can reap its rewards.

9

The Business Case for a Learning Culture

B y now, you have a pretty solid grasp on the what, why, and how of building a thriving learning culture at your workplace. But you know you can't effect change of this magnitude on your own or even with the support of a passionate L&D team behind you.

Before your leaders can signal the value of learning, as we described in Chapter 8, they need to make a real investment in it. That mostly means setting aside a chunk of budget, but it's not only about money. Even when leaders claim to see the upside of building a robust L&D function within their organizations, they don't always put enough resources behind it or give it enough time and runway to prove its worth. If your company's decision makers support L&D in theory, but in practice they aren't funding it at the levels you need, I have some ammo you can use.

Investing in L&D requires more than buying a bunch of licenses for a content platform, even one as great as Udemy for Business. Effective L&D requires a fundamental reimagining of how people approach their jobs and talk about performance, how managers and direct reports prioritize and discuss career development, and how the entire organization weighs risk and assesses capabilities.

A lot of this conversation is already happening in consultancies, think tanks, media outlets, and results-driven organizations: external forces are shining a bright light on thorny issues related to digital transformation, reskilling and upskilling, remote workforces, hiring and retention, and the future of work. Still, we're seeing a lag between company leaders recognizing these new conditions and stepping up to invest fully in L&D to mitigate the fallout. I was struck by the Accenture chief technology officer quoted in a *Wall Street Journal* article as saying, "Executives have this idea that 'as my people become obsolete, I'll just hire new people.' Well, they won't be there."[1]

Consider this: a 2018 McKinsey Global Institute report found that "sixty-two percent of executives believe they will need to retrain or replace more than a quarter of their workforce between now and 2023."[2] Awareness of the problem is a great starting point, but the McKinsey report also contained this sobering finding: "Only 16 percent of private-sector business leaders in this group feel 'very prepared' to address potential skills gaps, with roughly twice as many feeling either 'somewhat unprepared' or 'very unprepared.' The majority felt 'somewhat prepared'—hardly a clarion call of confidence."

Understandably, corporate leaders want assurance that any L&D investment will yield the desired results: a workforce equipped with the most relevant and business-critical skills, improved business performance, and increased employee engagement and retention. And not every company is an AT&T or JPMorgan Chase with an appetite for long-term experimentation or the ability to absorb risk as the business figures out the best way to reorganize around a learning culture. In the same *Wall Street Journal* article mentioned earlier, Erik Brynjolfsson, director of the Initiative on the Digital Economy at MIT, explains, "It's one thing to invest in machine learning; it's another to reinvent an organization or a business model. . . . Human capital is quantitatively a much bigger share of the capital in the economy than physical assets like plants, technology and equipment, and we understand it less well."

Learning and Development ROI Is Squishy; We Know This

It's hard enough to measure the impact of a marketing campaign, even with quantifiable metrics such as impressions, click-throughs, engagement, and time on site, before you even reach the holy grail of conversions, revenue, and growth. Indeed, digital transformation has turned most of our organizations into data-driven operations that constantly check the numbers and use them to optimize their processes. We can fine-tune everything from how frequently we send email to which color we make the call-to-action button, to which elements we emphasize in product demos.

Because learning is a purely human activity (even when facilitated through technology), and a highly individualized one at that, it's obviously harder to assign specific, unchanging performance metrics. How do we definitively know the learning objectives have been achieved? How do you determine whether Employee A has learned a new skill or that he or she has done it X percent "better" than Employee B? And how do you translate Employee A's effective learning into business impact? How can you prove causation versus correlation?

Plenty of measurement frameworks and ROI models have been bouncing around the L&D space for decades. They're not always compelling or speedy enough to make the case for an investment in learning. For now, companies need to take at least some of learning's return on faith, even as they see real, hard numbers indicating the urgency to upskill or reskill their workforces. L&D needs to tell an effective story with compelling examples to sell the narrative that a culture of on-demand, employee-driven, continuous learning will support business objectives.

Presenting Learning and Development to the C-Suite

When I meet with company executives to discuss the value of learning, I start my pitch by explaining the risks and opportunities shaping the modern workplace and why investing in L&D to build a robust learning culture makes sense. I lay out four specific reasons companies and the individuals within them will benefit from this change.

FIGURE 9.1 Current business challenges driving adoption of learning and development

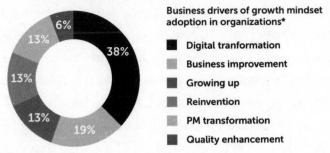

Business drivers of growth mindset adoption in organizations*

- Digital tranformation
- Business improvement
- Growing up
- Reinvention
- PM transformation
- Quality enhancement

*Percentage of organizations in our sample that adopt growth mindset to fulfill the listed objectives. Percentages add up to 102% due to rounding.

(Industry research, NeuroLeadership Institute, 2018)

1. A Learning Culture Is Critical for Keeping Up with Workplace Transformation

As we see from Figure 9.1, skills training is more important than ever in today's fast-moving, ever-changing workplace, where automation and numerous other factors are transforming the way we do our jobs. Plenty of research shows that corporate leaders know this is happening, and some are starting to shift their budgets in that direction. The Association for Talent Development found that "direct training expenditures rose from $1,081 per employee in 2009 (the first year of the survey) to $1,273 in 2016. The U.S. ranks near the top of the global heap, with 66 percent of workers receiving training from employers in the past year, according to the Organization for Economic Cooperation and Development."[3]

But is this money being spent wisely? In this environment of rapid digital transformation, learning can't be an interruption that takes employees away from their work for chunks of time. Rather, it has to be woven into people's daily routine to help them perform their jobs and drive productivity. Companies that treat learning as a strategic asset understand this and make just-in-time learning resources easily available so people can pick up skills in the moment of need, apply what they've learned right away, and keep important projects moving forward.

But they don't stop there. They also have to help employees embrace a growth mindset, facilitate blended-learning programs, show real interest in employees' career goals (not just job performance), and operate in a way that's consistent with prioritizing learning as a "way to win."

2. A Learning Culture Can Help Close Your Own Skills Gap

With unemployment at historic lows, companies are struggling to find qualified workers to fill open positions.

The *2018 Udemy Skills Gap* report found that 84 percent of Americans believe the skills gap exists (up about 5 percent from the previous year), and 39 percent already feel personally impacted by it.[4] Most survey respondents told us their employers could do a lot more to connect people with suitable training. Udemy's research parallels what the US Chamber of Commerce Foundation has reported, too, including its finding that this gap persists across industries.[5]

The gap between the skills applicants have and the skills employers seek can't be resolved by sending everyone back to school. Even if you hire for today's must-have skills, that's no guarantee you'll have the right talent for tomorrow's.

Upskilling existing talent is far more cost-effective and efficient than continually recruiting and onboarding new hires. Besides, workers genuinely want access to learning opportunities—and they're willing to leave for new employment when they don't get it. One survey of workers by the American Psychological Association found that "only 15 percent say their employer provides opportunities for them to develop the technical skills they will need in the future, only 20 percent say their employer provides training in necessary 'soft skills,' such as teamwork and communication, and just 8 percent report having the opportunity to develop the necessary leadership and management skills."[6]

Udemy research backs this up, especially for the newest entrants to the workforce, millennials and Gen Z—that is, the people you should be grooming for increasing responsibility and management roles. While 36 percent of workers over age 38 said they would leave a job if they didn't receive necessary training, 66 percent of those between ages 18 and 37 said they would quit for a more invested employer.[7]

3. A Learning Culture Fuels Innovation

It doesn't matter what industry you're in, your company's future success depends on its ability to harness the power of emerging technologies like artificial intelligence and data science . . . and whatever comes after that. To do that, you'll need humans with the technical know-how for designing, deploying, and maintaining these systems as well as the soft skills for doing what machines can't.

In a learning culture, where upskilling is encouraged and available, employees are more likely to experiment and innovate. There aren't limits on what they can do when relevant training is right at their fingertips.

Here's a suggestion that might be a hard sell to the C-suite as well as some line-of-business managers: to bring fresh perspectives and ideas into your organization, try letting workers learn across functions. Cross-pollinating from one part of the business to another can surface opportunities as well as risks that the core team hadn't considered. When selling the learning culture idea up the food chain, you can talk about things like job rotations or even simple desk swaps that can spark idea sharing among groups and individuals who might not have connected otherwise. It's also a great way to ensure that a diverse array of people contributes their perspectives and experiences. As a bonus, these opportunities boost retention, so you don't have to go out looking for another hire with a certain skill set who's also hungry to keep learning.

Today's CEOs prize innovation and see it as critical to growth, but according to PwC research, 77 percent of them "find it difficult to get the creativity and innovation skills they need" and regard the skills gap as a threat to innovation.[8] L&D leaders need to communicate how a learning culture can help close that gap and spur innovation too.

4. There Are More Technologies Than Ever to Make a Learning Culture Possible

As I pointed out earlier, executives don't like vague reassurances that strategies will pay off and that workers will behave a certain way. They like solid hypotheses and goals, rigorous mechanisms for testing and measuring, and quantifiable outcomes that can be directly linked to business performance. It's hard to communicate all that when it comes to individual humans learning at their own speed.

But throughout this book we've discussed how and why L&D can no longer be delivered as a passive, one-way experience. This is even more true as we are all in an era of distributed, global workforces. We have more employees working remotely than ever before. Fortunately, we have many more technology tools and platforms at our disposal to give employees access to learning and give leaders insights into learning activities.

We can learn more now about how effective L&D is at changing worker behavior and how that translates into performance improvements.

Just look at what Walmart is doing in one specific area: using virtual reality "to judge how effectively someone might function in a new role with more responsibility" and determine if that employee is promotion ready.[9] According to Walmart's director of media relations, using VR technology doesn't just help spot leadership potential; it can also determine when someone might be suited for a different job entirely. The company says its VR training "improves employee confidence and has boosted test scores 10 to 15 percent." You can bet other companies are taking notice and will look at VR to reduce their own training costs while reaping better results.

In an interview with *HR Technologist*, Karen Hebert-Maccaro, the chief learning experience officer at O'Reilly Media, spoke eloquently about rapid advances in learning technology that are making it possible to deliver learning opportunities in a "performance-adjacent manner"—that is, as part of the regular workflow—"with minimal disruption and maximum relevance." She added, "The rise of technologies like natural language processing (can make search more precise) and voice interfaces (can mean asking for learning support without taking eyes off the workflow) enable this type of learning."[10]

Hebert-Maccaro went on to describe how other technologies not expressly designed for L&D purposes are also helping learners in the workplace. She cited voice-command assistants such as Alexa and Google Home and connected devices and wearables such as smartwatches as having the potential to enable microlearning whenever and wherever learners need access.

HOW PUBLICIS SAPIENT MAKES TIME FOR LEARNING

As a global digital agency that works with some of the world's leading brands, Publicis Sapient says its top priority is always delivering great work that meets clients' business objectives. As at most agencies, employees at Sapient are accountable for tracking their billable hours and staying above a certain "utilization rate," that is, spending the maximum of their time on client work.

That makes sense, considering that's how Sapient generates revenue, but it doesn't leave a lot of space for learning. When Ian Stevens, North American lead, Capability Development, arrived at Sapient, L&D primarily functioned as a delivery team responsible for onboarding and soft-skills training on things like how to give presentations. Learning and development wasn't aligned with Sapient's overall business strategy. Meanwhile, Sapient's clients (just like the agency itself) were contending with the forces of digital transformation, and they expected Sapient's workforce to possess the expertise and cutting-edge skills required for creating innovative digital experiences.

How could Sapient balance the need for employees to "stay billable" with the ongoing and increasingly critical need to upskill and reskill continuously? And how could the L&D team convince senior executives and client partners to give people additional time away from client work to spend on learning?

The program they developed was both a response to skills needed right away for current client engagements and anticipatory of skills Sapient would need to continue winning new business. Rather than attempt a complete overhaul of L&D, Stevens's team wisely opted to initially focus on a single much-in-demand technology area (artificial intelligence) and offer this opportunity to a group of employees with highly relevant roles.

To sell the idea to client service executives, Stevens was willing to compromise on just how many hours per week employees would engage in this targeted training in addition to the two to three hours per week they were already expected to pursue on their own. He readily admits the first cohort to go through the AI training program had a rocky experience. Client partners weren't exactly holding up their end of the bargain to support this redeployment of resources, and as a result, people weren't showing up for scheduled learning events.

Rather than escalate the issue to force client partners to stick with the program, Stevens engaged in more negotiation. He knew L&D would be better off maintaining robust, positive relationships with these folks over the long haul by showing them the benefits of the training program, not calling them out for lack of cooperation.

So, Stevens and his team forged ahead, and only three employees successfully completed the first full AI training program. But those three employees sent a strong signal to the rest of the organization, including the client partners. The learners were able to move into roles previously staffed by contractors, which saved money, and other employees noticed what they had accomplished and wanted in on the action. They, too, wanted to participate in programs that would grow their skill sets and qualify them for new, interesting projects at work.

By upskilling existing employees instead of looking outside for experienced contractors, Sapient would be able to draw from a deeper and broader pool of talent to staff projects and go after new business. But L&D had to be a strategic partner and work in alignment with agency leadership to craft more programs that fit Sapient's growth pipeline and projected future needs. Again, Stevens's team started small, first offering the training capabilities to one small account team, then two or three accounts as a cohort, and finally across industries. People paid attention. Immediately, there was more knowledge sharing, more discussion about skills and problem solving, and generally, a much stronger learning culture.

Stevens shared the following proof points for his business case:

- **Cost effectiveness.** Using our own people instead of paying expensive contractors helps Sapient's bottom line.
- **Improved engagement.** Less churn among contractors and lower employee turnover make the workforce more connected and committed to each other and to Sapient.
- **Motivated mindset.** Employees see opportunities to grow into new or better roles and want to take advantage, helping Sapient retain high-value, highly driven workers to deliver transformational client work.

These results supported Stevens's contention that L&D could be doing more from a strategic standpoint to grow Sapient's capabilities and solve real business problems. The intensive AI training program is still in its early stages, so Stevens and his team are just starting to collect and evaluate data. They're looking at all manner of metrics to demonstrate the program's value and, just as important, to continue refining, building, and improving it.

"When you're in a learning culture, you just know it. You don't need to track things like how many hours people spent on training as much as what people are saying and how they're feeling about the program," Stevens says. He's more interested to see how Sapient has been able to meet open needs without paying contractors, how having technical specialties (AI, cloud computing, data science, etc.) allows Sapient to do more and different work on behalf of clients, and how confident executives feel going into new business pitches knowing the agency has the skills to deliver on its promises. In addition, Stevens is looking at the data to see how L&D's work is impacting Sapient's attrition rate and whether program participants are getting better performance reviews and more promotions.

The L&D team also uses learner feedback to tailor the experience and continue to iterate on programs to better meet employees' needs and preferences. Specifically, Stevens wants to find themes or trends in the feedback, such as the drop-out rate or the number of people who complete the training on time. The feedback Stevens's team values "isn't so much about the content. It's about the experience and the engagement."[11] Those are insights that can be applied to many L&D initiatives to ensure employees have the time and space to derive maximum benefit but also, just as important, that they feel good about the learning experience and think it was something worthwhile that they want more of.

This new approach asks Sapient's managers to take a more active role in cultivating their people's skills and supporting their career development, whereas before they simply directed employees to L&D for whatever training was available. It's an ongoing adjustment, but Stevens and his team now have quantitative and qualitative results they can point to if a manager or client partner questions employees dedicating more time to learning activities.

Use the following tips to demonstrate the value of learning to leadership:

- **Start small.** Although they had far grander ambitions, Sapient kicked off its training with a single specialty, artificial intelligence. Stevens suggests aiming for a quick win that shows the L&D team is "scrappy and thinking outside the box in order to add value." Then, they won't have to prove themselves over and over again when they want more budget.

- **Be selective . . . initially.** Sapient didn't open up the AI training program to everyone at first; they were deliberate in identifying the employees for whom learning was most relevant and who could be quickly deployed on client work with their newly acquired skills. Those employees' early achievements were received well by leadership, but they also signaled to other employees what was possible if they, too, committed to the training.

- **Forge relationships.** L&D at Sapient knows that a learning culture must be built on trust. Stevens met with stakeholders to understand their business requirements as well as their concerns before designing the training or

> inviting employees to participate. They stayed flexible and worked together as partners, rather than being territorial about when and how people could learn.

Case Study: Calculating the ROI of Udemy for Business

To better understand the business impact of workplace learning, Udemy for Business commissioned the analyst firm IDC to help quantify the value of having a strategic learning partner like Udemy for Business. The result was the report "The ROI and Value of Udemy for Business for Corporate Learning."[13] Udemy for Business is a learning platform that helps companies stay competitive in today's rapidly changing workplace by offering fresh, relevant, on-demand learning content, curated from the Udemy marketplace. The goal is to help employees do whatever comes next—whether that's the next project to do, skill to learn, or role to master. IDC is a global provider of market intelligence, advisory services, and events for the information technology, telecommunications, and consumer technology markets.

IDC conducted in-depth conversations with Udemy for Business customers and analyzed both qualitative and quantitative data to determine the return on investment that organizations can realize by using the Udemy for Business platform.

IDC found that for every dollar spent on Udemy for Business, organizations could realize an 869 percent return on investment in three years, or nearly nine incremental or saved dollars for every dollar invested in Udemy for Business solutions. The IDC report also noted that participating Udemy for Business customers with an internal L&D strategy in place could break even on their investment within two months of deployment and experience a 10 percent increase in employee satisfaction rates.

In total, IDC calculated that Udemy for Business customers would achieve annual benefits worth $4.32 million per organization per year, or $5,191 per employee trained. Although those findings were specific to IDC's study of Udemy for Business, they support two of my assertions: that workplace learning is critical for employee productivity, innovation, and engagement, and that the right learning solution can deliver real value to the bottom line. Here's what IDC called out in evaluating Udemy for Business's benefits:

- Cost-effective licensing allows customers to extend the reach of their L&D efforts to more employees globally and connect them with high-quality training content.
- Targeted, relevant, and engaging content motivates employees to learn the right skills when they need them and not waste precious time looking for resources or sitting in irrelevant training.
- High-quality content taught by real-world experts improves employee performance at their jobs.

- Proprietary training content and other skills development courses included as part of the new-hire onboarding process helps employees achieve productivity faster.
- Organizations can satisfy core business metrics, including generating more revenue, by empowering employees to leverage available learning resources when they need to take on additional responsibilities, earn required certifications, and the like.

Obviously, Udemy represents only a single piece in a multipronged approach to creating a robust learning culture, but it helps to have a platform like ours as your foundation. And, when you're convincing the C-suite to invest in a solution like Udemy, you can assuage any budgetary concerns by demonstrating the cost-savings data (Figure 9.2).

FIGURE 9.2 Staff time required to take training courses

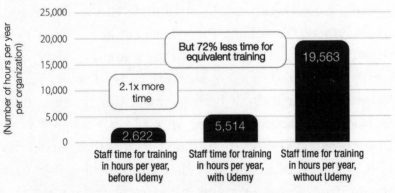

("The ROI and Value of Udemy for Business for Corporate Learning," document #US44873719, February 2019)

That's what the Udemy for Business customers in IDC's study expressed. For example, one said, "We can give employees the skills the next day rather than by the time the skill has moved on," and another customer liked having access to "agile and scrappy" content on whatever's hot in the business world at that moment.

In addition, a platform-based solution—like virtually all technology-enabled learning tools—provides managers and administrators with lots of data. That means senior executives don't have to wonder whether the services are being fully used by employees. User analytics and feedback can help connect the dots between "I used this resource to learn X and do Y" and "Our business was able to hit its goals for the quarter."

What Learning and Development Can—or Can't—Measure Matters

There's a well-worn quote attributed to the renowned management consultant Peter Drucker that "what gets measured gets managed." Or, to put it another way, what can be measured is what businesses tend to focus on. When we talked about how to make the business case to leadership about investing in L&D, we covered how important it is to show quantifiable results that impact the bottom line. Metrics are also vital for informing how and where your learning programs can grow and improve.

Of course, you have to start by defining the objectives of any learning initiatives so you'll know what to measure your results against. If you can't articulate success metrics for a given initiative, you shouldn't be doing it. And tracking more metrics isn't necessarily a goal. You want to be measuring the *right* things, which will be informed by your overall learning strategy.

Now, a big caveat: Not everything that matters *can* be measured. The gut instincts that come with experience and expertise shouldn't be discounted, even if they can't be quantified. People should be able to leverage their expertise to advocate for a certain strategy or approach, and L&D teams should be given leeway to trust their instincts based on experience.

L&D and HR teams have too often been dismissed by business leaders because we haven't done a good job demonstrating both where our expertise matters and where we have metrics. Fortunately, people analytics are becoming more sophisticated. The future of learning lies in combining data sets, finding trends, and understanding better how people interact with each other and technology. This is the holy grail of L&D: having data that shows that the work of the L&D team directly drives performance improvements. For example, people managers who complete a manager program score significantly better in reviews, and you can point to those results to encourage more learning activity.

What's key is that you don't just look back at what happened but reflect on what you've learned and what could have been better. The data needs to move you forward. Udemy's own product uses machine learning to anticipate a learner's ongoing needs and recommend the course or courses he or she should take next. You should apply predictive analytics to support your employees and, more generally, to keep your team focused on the company's most pressing needs.

Evaluate, Then Integrate

The insightful nuggets you gain from analytics will mean nothing if they're not integrated into your workplace culture and kept top of mind. The mindset of the L&D team (and, by extension, the whole company) has to be one of continuous improvement so that metrics don't get the "one and done" treatment and learning doesn't happen as a series of one-off events. Instead, your learning culture should add up to more than the sum of its parts.

For example, are you collecting data that could help managers have more robust career conversations with their direct reports? What about the ecosystem around your facilitated learning events? Go back to our mention of the scaffolding concept in Chapter 2 and make sure you're collecting feedback and outcomes that validate (or not) how you're connecting learning experiences to move people forward and keep them actively engaged over time.

10

Care and Maintenance of Your Learning Culture

We have now established that learning cultures are living organisms populated by real humans. They need everyone's participation and support, or they'll stagnate. At the same time, learning cultures require freshness and renewed energy to avoid stagnancy. In other words, a learning culture is not a "set it and forget it" initiative:

- There are always new employees cycling into your organization. Ideally, they've been hired because they have demonstrated learning agility and a growth mindset, and they've been introduced to your learning culture and their role in it during the onboarding process. L&D team members and managers need to keep an eye on newcomers to make sure they understand what learning is available to them and how important it is to stay actively learning.

- Your existing employees may be having awesome learning experiences today, but they'll need new inspiration and motivation over time. Even the best programs can become stale if they're not revisited and updated. Your trainers and facilitators will tire of delivering the same thing indefinitely, too. Post-training surveys and other feedback can help you identify opportunities for ongoing improvement and reinvention.

- The most sought-after hard skills are always changing; today's hot programming language is tomorrow's obsolete code. Soft skills, such as leadership or problem solving, might seem like they would stay fairly consistent over time, but that's not true either. As your organization grows, you may need different types of leadership, and as your business evolves, you will have to solve different kinds of problems. Your learning culture needs to adapt to these changes.

- We're seeing advances in technology all the time, from AI and machine learning to virtual reality and augmented reality. Those tools might not fit your learning culture today, but your team should stay abreast of the latest developments and be ready to act when a new technology emerges that can help you deliver learning content in more effective, engaging ways.

- Remember Chapter 2? We are still learning about learning. I know that's true of me as an L&D leader, but it's also true of our entire industry. One of the coolest parts of attending so many industry events and conferences is getting to see how knowledge is shared among professionals. What one company has been doing for years might be a brand-new concept to a start-up. And our assumptions about brain science are always being refined (if not outright debunked).[1] There's always new insight into how we can get better in our jobs.

I hope this book has left you itching to get out there and implement new strategies and programs for launching and growing your organization's learning culture. But before you put it back on the shelf, here's some advice for the longer term.

Establish Accountability

You should be on the lookout for a few areas of caution as your learning culture gains steam. I love when people are so inspired by the work of the L&D team that they want *more* learning programs and content and start organically creating meaningful learning experiences on their own. To me, this is a hallmark of a true learning culture.

But keeping tabs on duplicative or misaligned initiatives is also important. Enthusiasm is a good thing . . . until it isn't. When anyone and everyone is developing learning programs independently—for their specific teams, around a specific company initiative, in support of a new tool or process—it can occasionally add up to duplicated, misspent time and effort. It can lead to inconsistencies in how a program or initiative is perceived and delivered across the organization. It can make it hard to access the learning you need at the moment you need it. Many large organizations struggle with this challenge. And it can also undermine the principles and values upon which your learning culture is based.

Rather than play an endless and counterproductive game of whack-a-mole, you'll need to establish a philosophy and strategy around supporting democratized learning activities. At the least, you need to stay visible and approachable. I know I'm repeating myself, but this is another situation where your early investment in relationship building will pay off. When people trust you and have seen how you add value to their work, they'll be more likely to come to you with their ideas first—not to ask permission, necessarily, but to get your help and advice. Or they may be more likely to check and see if something already exists that could be used. Conversely, if your L&D team has a reputation for always saying no, pushing people to conform to process, standing in the way, or slowing them down, that has to be addressed first.

Most of the time, these employee-led initiatives are exciting, positive signals of your culture. But there are occasionally times when you'll want to step in and get involved. For example, at Udemy, my team was working on a companywide interview training when I caught wind that a team was building its own workshop on this topic. This particular workshop was pretty significant to the company—we had huge growth plans for the coming year and knew we had to support the company in effective hiring. This other team was innocently working on the same problem because their department was feeling the same pain. Luckily we heard about the initiative early and were able to partner to make sure we were taking into account the recruiting team's best practices.

But L&D does need to intervene in plenty of instances. I want to be clear that our job isn't to police behavior, control others, or give permission but rather to ensure these activities are aligned with our strategic plans and priorities, don't overlap with our own work, and make sense as part of our learning culture. You may even find that a "rogue" idea would be better if it were expanded more broadly around the organization, so it makes sense to get involved. The L&D team knows how to make these programs succeed.

I can almost guarantee where you'll find lots of employee-led initiatives: in satellite locations. Especially if your company has L&D staff only at headquarters, you shouldn't be surprised when people in other offices do their own thing. Your team needs to be thoughtful about communicating with remote workers or global offices. Consider making more frequent visits to their locations to strengthen those relationships. The fact is, it's the L&D

team's responsibility to develop all employees regardless of their location, and I suggest approaching it in the spirit of partnership. That's what we've done with Udemy's workforce in Dublin, Ankara, Denver, and elsewhere. The best way to get yourself excluded from L&D discussions in those remote offices is to stifle everything they want to try.

Here's an example of where L&D and employee groups can work together. Udemy's Culture Crew is a group of employees who have volunteered to plan fun, engaging events and activities that support and promote our company culture. They had the idea of trying an internal mentorship program, something that was already on the L&D road map. We didn't ask them to stop; we partnered with them to test it. We provided up-front guidance and advice and worked with the Culture Crew to lead a series of pilot workshops with employees. We're using the results of this pilot to move mentorships into a companywide initiative. This was a win for everyone: the voice of the Culture Crew was heard and valued, and the L&D team got a jump start on work we would have done anyway.

Building Out Your Learning and Development Team's Offerings and Services

One aspect of thinking like a marketer is keeping your content fresh. When things stay too much the same, we stop noticing them (like that bag of clothes I've been meaning to donate, which has been sitting by the front door for months and doesn't even register with me anymore).

When thinking of opportunities to broaden your services, don't be tempted to forge ahead with new content and changes without doing your strategy work. You need to keep your learners' needs and interests as your guiding light. A good place to start, especially for newer L&D organizations, is the employee life cycle itself. Consider the arc that starts with recruiting. It's hard to identify rigid career paths anymore, but we can still equip people with appropriate skills as they take on new responsibilities, move into management, embark on a different kind of project, or start working with a new team. That's why we're building a specific So, You Want to Be a Manager? workshop available to anyone. Our leadership content is targeted to people who've already risen through the ranks, those who still aspire to leadership, and others who may not even be sure what their options are. We're doing this because, even if someone has stayed in the same role for a period of time without complaint, a conversation with L&D or a manager can reveal areas ripe for development, especially around soft skills.

Leadership development was an area PCL targeted when it looked at places its L&D culture needed to grow. "Originally, it was geared to the top 1 percent of the company—our highest performers and high potentials," Mike Olsson explains. "Now, we have leadership development programs for all PCLers at all levels of the organization. And they are not cookie-cutter. They are big-time investments into creating an opportunity to help people be better leaders, better managers, better citizens, better parents and spouses."

Sometimes the updates will be obvious: a new or revised course that captures the most recent iteration of the Python programming language or training around a new tool being deployed for product prototyping. You should also be culling your L&D programs regularly to remove any obsolete content so employees don't use it unwittingly.

Soft skills, of course, are always in style, but employees will be at different stages of mastery. Leverage your relationships across the organization to keep abreast of where soft skills are too, umm, soft. You may find that what had been sufficiently addressed in a self-paced course now needs more hands-on facilitation and guidance. If your company is growing superfast or experiencing other big changes, a new needs assessment yearly or even more frequently is a good idea.

Speaking of growing head count, the size of your company could create different learning needs. Employees who came on board when you were a scrappy 30-person start-up might need extra support finding their purpose when head count numbers are in the hundreds or thousands. Growing companies often have to reorganize themselves at the department or team level, and that can be nerve-wracking. Managers need to be trained to lead people through transition periods. If you're not already offering change management workshops, trainings, and role-playing, you should give it serious thought.

Maintaining Your Culture's Health

Having solid, trusting relationships around the company is the best way to get honest feedback on how your L&D team and programs are doing. You know you're doing it right when people come to you voluntarily to talk about a learning experience they've had—good or bad—and to share ideas about new training they would love to have available.

But many, perhaps most, employees aren't going to approach you with unsolicited feedback. You need to go to them. At Udemy, we send out a survey after every workshop and webinar. Our online courses, too, have mechanisms for students to provide ratings and share comments. We look at all of this, regularly and with open minds. As much as I and my team know about instructional design and learning science, we never presume to know better than our students what works best for them, where they're hitting challenges, what topics need deeper treatment, and so on.

I'm not saying we're awesome just because we send out surveys. I get why surveys are denigrated as "smile sheets" if they're only used to validate where we were right or did something good. I assure you, however, my L&D team really listens to feedback and strives to address people's concerns and suggestions.

In fact, I credit my husband, Tom, for helping me instill a continuous improvement mindset in Udemy's L&D team. Tom is a software engineer, and he taught me all about how he runs his teams by following an agile software development approach. The agile methodology is a collaborative and iterative process that encourages flexibility, which is no small matter in a fast-moving, always-changing workplace.

We don't apply every aspect of the agile methodology to L&D, but some of its foundational concepts have been helpful to ensure we're headed in the right direction and to maintain that forward momentum.

Specifically, I urge everyone to embrace the maxim that "the perfect is the enemy of the good." None of us is ever perfect. Better to accept it and move on rather than get bogged down while other projects languish on your to-do list. This can be frustrating for people who like to check things off and know they're finished. With agile development, nothing is ever "final." We are always improving, reinventing, and iterating—because conditions are always changing.

Another agile methodology concept that tends to get universal agreement is that quality is our brand. We constantly strive toward doing better. Because we're in service to the organization, we're committed to delivering experiences that satisfy our growing and changing workforce. What we've done before might have been suitable then, but it might not be right for today. And the L&D team does not decide alone whether we've hit our quality standards; it's our learners.

I find it interesting that this attitude is reflected among the most successful instructors on the Udemy platform. Although many create online courses hoping to earn substantial revenue (and lots of them do), the most popular instructors are actually those who have a passion for their subject and an authentic desire to help others by sharing knowledge. They're also the ones who are most engaged with their students by answering questions, giving extra advice, and making sure their content is up-to-date. Instructors who are mainly in it to enrich themselves, who think they can publish a course and then sit back and watch it grow, often come away dissatisfied.

To build and maintain a learning culture, your L&D team members had better love what they do and embrace constructive feedback on their performance. If you've started by defining your goals and key performance indicators, you can design surveys to surface exactly the type of information that will help you understand where you're doing well and where opportunities for improvement exist.

Hiring for Agility and Growth Mindset

To maintain the integrity and strength of your learning culture, it's important to evaluate potential new hires through a learning lens too. Basically, you want to be on the lookout for agile, adaptable learners who will add to your culture and who won't be at odds with your expectations that all employees continuously learn and grow. Without a doubt, screening for potential and not simply reviewing a candidate's past accomplishments can be difficult, but competency-based interviews are becoming more common in direct response to the upskilling imperative.

At PCL Construction, Mike Olsson told me, "We do look for lifelong learners but don't really look for evidence of 'education' in the résumé. Instead, we focus on the candidate's different experiences and exposures and specifically ask for examples of that." By asking behavioral interview questions, PCL aims to identify those "who have had the right mindset, approach, and attitude that's gotten them through a challenge and over an obstacle."[2] These types of hires are receptive to the learning culture that's instilled when they join PCL and are eager to take part in the mentoring and career development that's core to what the company is.

What are some good behavior interview questions that might help you spot an agile learner? I'm glad you asked because I keep a running list:

- Tell me about a time when a project or idea didn't work. What did you do? What did you learn?
- What skills are you hoping to develop in this role?
- What skills did you develop in your last role?
- What do you see as your top skill, and how did you learn it?
- Tell me about a time you took on a role or project you weren't 100 percent prepared for. What did you do? How did you set yourself up for success?
- What have you learned from your current teammates or manager?
- Tell me about a time when you were given feedback you weren't expecting. How did you handle it?
- Tell me about a time when you successfully implemented feedback from others into your work.

As you can see, these questions don't let the interviewee get away with recounting past events or skirting the issue of exactly how and what they contributed. You have to dig a layer or two deeper to get at the candidate's mindset and attitude and determine how they react to setbacks as well as successes.

A Few Thoughts on How Diversity Fits In

I'm a firm believer that diversity initiatives cannot exist in a vacuum; they have to be woven into everything happening within an organization. Negative forces like unconscious bias can undermine work at any juncture, so mindfulness and sensitivity need to move to the fore at all times.

What does that mean in a learning culture? Of course, mindfulness and sensitivity mean delivering training around relevant topics, such as the aforementioned unconscious bias, as well as psychological safety (how managers can foster this in their teams), allyship (building relationships that promote an inclusive culture), and self-advocacy (helping people get comfortable speaking up and expressing their needs constructively).

Although I have previously written that it's counterproductive to make training mandatory, DEI (diversity/equity/inclusiveness) is an area where I think all employees should be expected to complete the programs. On the tactical side, learning content and activities themselves need to reflect inclusive values. Instructional design should take into consideration a diversity of participants and not simply "obvious" demographics like race or gender. Think about the kinds of people you show in presentations or tell stories about. Have you included all kinds of people and not just those who mirror your workforce? Think about the format of your learning programs. Have you accommodated the needs of people with disabilities or who speak other languages or who are simply introverts who shy away from speaking up in a group setting? Are there any messages in the training, implied or explicit, that could alienate, offend, or disturb a learner? When these situations do arise, they're rarely malicious, which is why I prioritized unconscious bias so deliberately at Udemy. Without that baseline awareness, your otherwise great training can fail to produce the desired outcome.

Finally, within the context of diversity and inclusiveness, I'll return to something I brought up earlier in this book: democratizing learning by making it available to your entire workforce. I wish I could remember who said it, but I often think about a line I heard at a TED-Ed talk that went like this: "Access to education should be as available as access to an elevator."

That's an excellent note to end on. Maintaining the health of your learning culture is about expanding the importance and role of learning in your organization, not shrinking it. Anything you do as an L&D practitioner should start from a place of inclusion, empowerment, and service to the organization—the *whole* organization.

Companies aren't static entities. They're made up of living, breathing humans. Business can be unpredictable; people can be unpredictable. Grounding your culture in learning and development is the surest way to navigate through changes, whether they originate inside or outside the organization.

NOTES

CHAPTER 1

1. Lynda Gratton and Andrew Scott, *The 100-Year Life: Living and Working in an Age of Longevity*, London: Bloomsbury Publishing, 2016, http://www.100yearlife.com/.
2. "Careers and Learning: Real Time, All the Time," in *2017 Global Human Capital Trends*, February 28, 2017, Deloitte Insights, https://www2.deloitte.com/insights/us/en/focus/human -capital-trends/2017/learning-in-the-digital-age.html.
3. David Mallon, *High-Impact Learning Culture: The 40 Best Practices for Creating an Empowered Enterprise*, Bersin & Associates Research Report, June 2010, https://joshbersin.com/2010/06 /how-to-build-a-high-impact-learning-culture/.
4. "Labor Force Projections to 2024: The Labor Force Is Growing, but Slowly," *Monthly Labor Review*, December 2015, Bureau of Labor Statistics, https://www.bls.gov/opub/mlr/2015/article /labor-force-projections-to-2024.htm.
5. *2018 Skills Gap Report*, Udemy, 2018, https://research.udemy.com /research_report/2018-skill-gap-report/.
6. *Udemy in Depth: 2018 Millennials at Work Report*, Udemy, 2018, https://research.udemy.com/research_report/udemy-in-depth -2018-millennials-at-work-report/.

CHAPTER 2

1. Praveen Shrestha, "Ebbinghaus Forgetting Curve," *Psychestudy*, November 2017, https://www.psychestudy.com/cognitive /memory/ebbinghaus-forgetting-curve.
2. William Thalheimer, *Spacing Learning Over Time: What the Research Says*," Work-Learning Research, 2006.
3. "Learning Styles Debunked: There Is No Evidence Supporting Auditory and Visual Learning, Psychologists Say," *Association for Psychological Science*, December 2009,

https://www.psychologicalscience.org/news/releases/learning
-styles-debunked-there-is-no-evidence-supporting-auditory
-and-visual-learning-psychologists-say.html.

4. Jeffrey R. Young, "A Conversation with Bill Gates About the Future of Higher Education," *Chronicle of Higher Education*, June 25, 2012, https://www.chronicle.com/article/A-Conversation -With-Bill-Gates/132591.

5. Richard E. Clark, "Reconsidering Research on Learning from Media," *Review of Educational Research*, 53, no. 4 (Winter 1983): 445–459, http://www.uky.edu/~gmswan3/609/Clark_1983.pdf.

6. The Science of Classroom Design, infographic, USC Rossier School of Education, 2015, https://rossieronline.usc.edu/science -of-classroom-design-infographic/?utm_source=social&utm _medium=social.

7. Saul McLeod, "What Is the Zone of Proximal Development?" *Simply Psychology*, updated 2019, https://www.simplypsychology .org/Zone-of-Proximal-Development.html.

8. Nancy Duarte, Slide:ology: *The Art and Science of Creating Great Presentations*, Sebastopol, CA: O'Reilly Media, 2008.

9. Ricardo Schütz, "Stephen Krashen's Theory of Second Language Acquisition," March 2005, https://apps.esc1.net /ProfessionalDevelopment/uploads/WKDocs/58121/2.%20Stephen%20 Krashen.pdf.

10. Abraham Maslow, *Toward a Psychology of Being*, Princeton, NJ: Van Nostrand-Reinhold, 1962.

11. Fogg Behavior Model, https://www.behaviormodel.org/.

12. Yu-kai Chou, Octalysis—The Complete Gamification Framework, https://yukaichou.com/gamification-examples/octalysis -complete-gamification-framework/.

13. "Communicative Language Teaching," *Wikipedia*, https://en .wikipedia.org/wiki/Communicative_language_teaching.

14. "Andragogy (Malcolm Knowles)," InstructionalDesign.org, https://www.instructionaldesign.org/theories/andragogy/.

CHAPTER 3

1. Beth Davies, Connor Diemand-Yauman, and Nick van Dam, *Competitive Advantage with a Human Dimension: From Lifelong Learning to Lifelong Employability*, McKinsey & Company, February 2019, https://www.mckinsey.com/featured-insights/future

-of-work/competitive-advantage-with-a-human-dimension
-from-lifelong-learning-to-lifelong-employability.
2. Emily Ross, Bill Schaninger, Emily Seng Yue, *Right-skilling Your Future Workforce*, McKinsey & Company, August 2018, https://www.mckinsey.com/business-functions/organization/our-insights/the-organization-blog/right-skilling-for-your-future-workforce.
3. Valerie Bolden-Barrett, "Study: Turnover Costs Employers $15,000 per Worker," *HR Dive*, August 11, 2017, https://www.hrdive.com/news/study-turnover-costs-employers-15000-per-worker/449142/.
4. *2018 Udemy Skills Gap Report*, Udemy, 2018, https://research.udemy.com/research_report/2018-skill-gap-report/.
5. Hilary Scarlett, *Neuroscience for Organizational Change: An Evidence-Based Practical Guide to Managing Change*, London: Kogan Page, 2016.
6. Phone and email interview with Mike Olsson, vice president of human resources and learning development at PCL, September 13, 2019.

CHAPTER 4

1. Center for the New Economy and Society, *The Future of Jobs Report 2018*, World Economic Forum, 2018, http://www3.weforum.org/docs/WEF_Future_of_Jobs_2018.pdf.
2. Modern Elder Academy, https://www.modernelderacademy.com/.
3. Phone and email interviews with Dana Alan Koch and Allison M. Horn, October 21, 2019, and January 29, 2020.
4. Tracking of formal learning hours not inclusive of on-the-job, in-the-flow-of-work learning.
5. "It's Learning. Just Not As We Know It," Accenture, https://www.accenture.com/_acnmedia/thought-leadership-assets/pdf/accenture-education-and-technology-skills-research.pdf.

CHAPTER 5

1. *Udemy in Depth: 2018 Millennials at Work Report*, Udemy, 2018, https://research.udemy.com/research_report/udemy-in-depth-2018-millennials-at-work-report/.

2. What Got You Here Won't Get You There: How Successful People Become Even More Successful, Marshall Goldsmith, https://www.marshallgoldsmith.com/product/book-2/.
3. "Randy Pausch," *Wikipedia*, https://en.wikipedia.org/wiki/Randy_Pausch.
4. Carol Dweck, *Mindset: The New Psychology of Success,* New York: Ballantine Books, 2007.
5. *Idea Report: Growth Mindset Culture*, NeuroLeadership Institute, 2018.

CHAPTER 6

1. *The Human Touch Drives Onboarding Success*, ADP, 2017, https://www.adp.com/resources/articles-and-insights/articles/t/the-human-touch-drives-onboarding-success.aspx#acForm.
2. Pokémon Go, *Wikipedia*, https://en.wikipedia.org/wiki/Pok%C3%A9mon_Go.
3. Britt Andreatta, *Wired to Grow: Harness the Power of Brain Science to Learn and Master Any Skill,* Santa Barbara, CA: 7th Mind Publishing, 2019.

CHAPTER 7

1. "Challenges Leaders Are Facing: The Frontline Leadership Project," 2018 Global Leadership Forecast, DDI, 2018, https://www.ddiworld.com/frontlineleaderproject/challenges-leaders-are-facing
2. Udemy, *What Motivates Employees to Learn*, San Francisco: Udemy, 2017.
3. "Supervisor Support Critical to Employee Well-Being and Workforce Readiness," American Psychological Association, October 18, 2017, https://www.apa.org/news/press/releases/2017/10/employee-well-being.
4. "Effects of Hunger on Education," The Borgen Project, July 2014, https://borgenproject.org/effects-of-hunger-on-education/.

CHAPTER 8

1. Tera Allas, Louis Chambers, and Tom Welchman, "Confronting Overconfidence in Talent Strategy, Talent Development, and Recruitment," McKinsey & Co., June 2019, https://www.mckinsey.com/featured-insights/future-of-work

/confronting-overconfidence-in-talent-strategy-management -and-development.

2. Phone and email interview with Mike Olsson, vice president of human resources and learning development at PCL, September 13, 2019.

3. "Challenges Leaders Are Facing: The Frontline Leader Project," 2018 Global Leadership Forecast, DDI, 2018, https://www .ddiworld.com/frontlineleaderproject/challenges-leaders-are -facing.

4. Interview with Darren Shimkus, president of Udemy for Business, San Francisco, CA, October 22, 2019.

CHAPTER 9

1. Lauren Weber, "Why Companies Are Failing at Reskilling," *The Wall Street Journal*, April 19, 2019, https://www.wsj.com/articles /the-answer-to-your-companys-hiring-problem-might-be-right -under-your-nose-11555689542.

2. Pablo Illanes, Susan Lund, Mona Mourshed, Scott Rutherford, and Magnus Tyreman, *Retraining and Reskilling Workers in the Age of Automation*, McKinsey & Company, January 2018, https://www .mckinsey.com/featured-insights/future-of-work/retraining -and-reskilling-workers-in-the-age-of-automation.

3. Peter Coy, "Now Is Not a Good Time to Skimp on Worker Training," October 2018, *BloombergQuint*, https://www .bloombergquint.com/business/now-is-not-a-good-time-to -skimp-on-worker-training.

4. *2018 Udemy Skills Gap*, Udemy, 2018, https://research.udemy.com /research_report/2018-skill-gap-report/.

5. Burning Glass Technologies, *Different Skills, Different Gaps: Measuring and Closing the Skills Gap*, US Chamber of Commerce Foundation, March 2018, https://www.uschamberfoundation .org/reports/different-skills-different-gaps-measuring-and -closing-skills-gap.

6. "2017 Job Skills Training and Career Development Survey," American Psychological Association, October 2017, http://www .apaexcellence.org/assets/general/2017-training-survey-results .pdf.

7. *2018 Udemy Skills Gap Report*, Udemy, 2018, https://research .udemy.com/research_report/2018-skill-gap-report/.

8. "The Talent Challenge: Harnessing the Power of Human Skills in the Machine Age," PwC, 2011, https://www.pwc.com/gx/en/ceo-survey/2017/deep-dives/ceo-survey-global-talent.pdf.
9. "Walmart Has Added Virtual Reality to Its Assessment of an Employee's Potential," *Washington Post*, July 12, 2019, https://www.washingtonpost.com/technology/2019/07/12/walmarts-latest-tool-assessing-whether-employees-deserve-promotion-virtual-reality/.
10. Radhika Mukherjee, "The Possibilities of Technology-Enabled Learning: An Interview with Karen Hebert-Maccaro of O'Reilly Media," *HR Technologist*, December 2018, https://www.hrtechnologist.com/interviews/learning-development/interview-oreilly-media-technology-enabled-learning/.
11. Phone and email interview with Ian Stevens, North American lead, capability development, at Publicis Sapient, November 11, 2019.
12. "The ROI and Value of Udemy for Business for Corporate Learning," IDC Document #US44873719, February 2019, https://business.udemy.com/resources/how-udemy-for-business-delivers_869_roi/.

CHAPTER 10

1. "The Problem with 'Learning Styles,'" *Scientific American*, May 2018, https://www.scientificamerican.com/article/the-problem-with-learning-styles/.
2. Phone and email interview with Mike Olsson, vice president of human resources and learning development at PCL, September 13, 2019.

INDEX

ABOUT THE AUTHOR

Shelley Osborne is passionate about creating corporate learning cultures that enable continuous skills development and nurture a growth mindset to drive employee engagement and company performance. She has over fifteen years of experience across the education, consulting, and corporate sectors.

Currently, Shelley is the Vice President of Learning at Udemy, where she leads the company's learning strategy and continuous upskilling of over 600 employees globally. In her work, she often leverages innovative technologies and fresh approaches like virtual reality and gamification to drive lasting engagement. Before Udemy, Shelley was the Vice President of Learning & Development at Farside HR Solutions, where she advised early- and late-stage companies on learning and talent strategy, skill development, and leadership programs. Before moving into the professional learning and development space, Shelley had a successful career as a classroom teacher in Canada for almost a decade. Today, she teaches on the Udemy platform and over 15,000 students are enrolled in her courses spanning topics such as how to give and receive feedback, growing as a manager, and others.

Shelley speaks regularly at industry events such as TED-Women, ATD International Conference, DevLearn, and Unleash. She contributes to numerous publications, including *Entrepreneur*, *Fast Company*, and the U.S. Chamber of Commerce Foundation. Shelley has also provided expert commentary for *The Wall Street Journal*, CNBC, Cheddar TV, *Inc.*, and more.

THE LEARNING IS JUST GETTING STARTED!

Join Shelley and over 100,000 Udemy students for one of her online courses. You'll learn how to give better feedback, manage teams, work remotely, and adapt to change. Her latest Udemy course delves more deeply into the ideas from *The Upskilling Imperative* and takes you through a step-by-step plan for building a learning culture.

See the full list of Shelley's courses at:
bit.ly/udemy-shelley

Change Agility in the Workplace: Become a Change Agent
Shelley Osborne
Free

5 Ways to make Learning Core to the Way We Work
Shelley Osborne
Free

Fostering Psychological Safety & Belonging on Teams
Shelley Osborne
Free

Career Navigator: A Manager's Guide to Career Development
Shelley Osborne
Free

The Manager's Guide to Effective One on One Meetings
Shelley Osborne
Free

Udemy helps people everywhere pursue their dreams and reach their goals. Explore over 150,000 courses taught by over 57,000 expert instructors today.